The Economic Performance

of Public Investments

THE ECONOMIC PERFORMANCE
OF PUBLIC INVESTMENTS:

An Ex Post Evaluation
of Water Resources Investments

Robert H. Haveman

Published for Resources for the Future, Inc.
By The Johns Hopkins Press, Baltimore and London

361015

Resources for the Future is a nonprofit corporation for research and education in the
development, conservation, and use of natural resources and the improvement of the
quality of the environment. It was established in 1952 with the cooperation of the Ford
Foundation. Part of the work of Resources for the Future is carried out by its resident
staff; part is supported by grants to universities and other nonprofit organizations.
Unless otherwise stated, interpretations and conclusions in RFF publications are those
of the authors; the organization takes responsibility for the selection of significant sub-
jects for study, the competence of the researchers, and their freedom of inquiry.

Robert Haveman, a visiting scholar at RFF at the time this study was made, is Professor
of Economics at the University of Wisconsin. Charts and maps were drawn by Clare and
Frank Ford. The index was prepared by Helen Eisenhart.

RFF editors: Henry Jarrett, Vera W. Dodds, Nora E. Roots, Tadd Fisher.

Copyright © 1972 by The Johns Hopkins Press
All rights reserved
Manufactured in the United States of America

The Johns Hopkins Press, Baltimore, Maryland 21218
The Johns Hopkins Press Ltd., London

Library of Congress Catalog Card Number 77–184311
ISBN 0–8018–1333–6

CONTENTS

LIST OF TABLES

LIST OF FIGURES

Foreword

The assessment of public projects is a complex and difficult matter. The repercussions of public sector activities are often subtle and widely dispersed. Moreover, evaluation of these activities should properly reflect society's preferences, but often these preferences are neither self-evident nor directly measurable. Finally, program evaluation may be resisted by public agencies because it is viewed as a threat. Despite these difficulties, there has been a growing trend in government toward the assessment of public programs. The Planning, Programming, and Budgeting System of the Executive Branch has encouraged evaluative studies of this sort. And more recently, the General Accounting Office has undertaken such analyses at the behest of Congress.

Over the years, a substantial literature has accumulated that deals with public investment in natural resources development generally and with water development projects in particular. The well-known 1950 report of the Federal Inter-Agency River Basin Committee[1] was one of the early economic contributions to the literature on project evaluation. The "Green Book," as this document has come to be known, presented the rationale for benefit-cost analysis to water development projects. It thus provided a base line for scholars, agency officials, and others who have tried to elaborate a theory and methodology for benefit-cost analysis as an instrument in resource development planning.

Resources for the Future has participated in this effort to apply benefit-cost analysis to resource development. In 1957, RFF sponsored a study in which the concepts and methods of benefit-cost analysis were developed and applied in three case study situations. The resulting publication, *Multiple Purpose River Development*, by John Krutilla and Otto Eckstein, dem-

[1] *Proposed Practices for Economic Analysis of River Basin Projects*, prepared by the Subcommittee on Benefits and Costs of the Federal Inter-Agency River Basin Committee.

xi

onstrated among other things the sensitivity of cost and benefit estimates to assumptions about the cost of public capital, as reflected in the rates of interest used for discounting future benefits and costs. More recently, Robert Haveman and John Krutilla examined the adequacy of benefit-cost analysis for evaluating projects during periods of less than full employment in both the national and regional economies. In this study, *Unemployment, Idle Capacity, and the Evaluation of Public Expenditures*, Haveman and Krutilla presented a methodology for tracing the incidence of water development resource demands generated by regions and by the sectors of the national economy.

In the present book, Robert Haveman extends this line of RFF work in an important dimension. His examination of the performance of a public project after it has been in operation deals with one of the weakest aspects of the planning process. Public resource development planning has been essentially a static ex ante activity. To be sure, the methodology and empirical planning factors have been improved over time, but few public resource agencies have developed procedures for monitoring the economic performance of the projects they have undertaken. Although the techniques for ex post project evaluation are far from perfected, Professor Haveman has presented a general framework within which additional empirical work can usefully be undertaken. Ultimately, the insights and quantitative information gained from ex post evaluation can be used by public authorities as planning guides for their subsequent decisions.

Although the book deals with water resource projects, the general framework for evaluation is applicable to other types of natural resources development. It is hoped that such studies will be made, modifying the analytical procedures where necessary, and that public activities in such areas as outdoor recreation, wildlife management, timber production, and highway development will benefit accordingly.

MICHAEL F. BREWER

Vice President
June 1971   *Resources for the Future*

Preface

As the role of the public sector in the United States economy expands relative to the private sector, it is essential that the tools of economic analysis and planning be applied to decisions in this sector. This necessity has been increasingly recognized since the techniques of benefit-cost analysis and cost effectiveness analysis have been developed. The federal government and state and local governments have established planning, programming, and budgeting systems to encourage the application of such analysis to proposed public actions. As a result, the economic effects of government programs are now more fully understood, and the necessity to initiate changes to increase the effectiveness of the public sector is more clearly perceived.

Nevertheless, the impact of analysis and evaluation on the quality of public decisions and the effectiveness of government performance has been small. Inefficient and inequitable public programs, apparently immune to evaluation or criticism, continue to thrive. Policy analysis and recommendations based on efficiency criteria are weak instruments with which to counteract vested power possessed by organized private interests receiving public subsidies, executive agencies administering programs, or legislative blocs "overseeing" government activities. If government is to perform in the public interest, incentives in the political system that favor such inefficiency and inequality must be altered.

Simultaneously with such political reform, however, it is necessary that the tools of policy analysis and planning continue to be developed and applied to public programs. While major progress has been made in applying efficiency and equity analysis to proposed public investment decisions, there has been little effort to evaluate the results of past policy actions. As a consequence, little is known of the accuracy of ex ante analytical techniques as applied by government agencies. Improvement in procedures for applying these techniques has not benefited from the feedback made possible by evaluating the performance of past projects.

This study is an exploratory effort to develop the techniques of ex post evaluation for water resources development activities. The range of project effects studied is limited to the direct benefits and costs, and these were analyzed for a small number of installations. It is hoped that this pilot study will stimulate additional efforts to improve the techniques of ex post evaluaation, to apply them to a wider range of public activities, and to employ the findings in improving the procedures for ex ante benefit-cost analysis.

In undertaking this study, I received the assistance of several persons. Terrill Langworthy and Paula Stephan worked as research assistants while they were students at Grinnell College, where much of the early work on this project was done. Chapter 5 is as much Mr. Langworthy's product as it is mine. In addition, I am indebted to several others who assisted in obtaining data and who provided technical assistance. These include Nathaniel Back and E. G. Long of the U.S. Army Corps of Engineers, Harry Wright of the Southeastern Power Administration, and Thomas Doran of the Board of Engineers for Rivers and Harbors. Helpful criticism of the manuscript was received from Blair Bower, Michael Brewer, and Walter Spofford of Resources for the Future, Inc.; David Allee of Cornell University; Emery Castle of Oregon State University; Maynard Hufschmidt of the University of North Carolina; A. Allan Schmid of Michigan State University; Robert Gidez and Jim Tozzi of the Corps of Engineers; and Edward Schiffers of the Board of Engineers for Rivers and Harbors. I also express my thanks to Charles Howe, former director of the Water Resources Program of Resources for the Future and now of the University of Colorado, who first interested me in this problem and who read and criticized the several incarnations of the study. Finally, the careful editing of Tadd Fisher is gratefully acknowledged.

April 1971   Robert H. Haveman

The Economic Performance

of Public Investments

CHAPTER 1

THE EX POST EVALUATION OF PUBLIC INVESTMENTS

In the literature of welfare economics, contributions to the theory and application of public expenditure analysis have grown rapidly in recent years. The economic efficiency, or national income maximization, criterion has become defined with precision, and the decision criteria pertinent to it have become specified, both with and without constraints. Similarly, there has been substantial progress in defining national income benefits and costs and in developing procedures for measuring them. And, even though there may not be unanimity among analysts, the range of approaches to the handling of uncertainty, time, and unemployment in the analysis of public expenditures has been substantially narrowed.[1]

In nearly all of this benefit-cost literature, emphasis has been placed on the ex ante evaluation of public expenditures. Attention has been focused on the decision maker, who, confronted with a set of alternatives, is required to choose a limited number from among them. Presuming that the decision maker desires to maximize the net economic benefits flowing from his decision, benefit-cost analysis has provided him with the conceptual tools required to discover the optimum set of alternatives on the basis of information known *prior* to the decision.

Only very recently has it been possible to find any significant research at all that focuses on the economic results of public undertakings after they have had time to develop a performance record. Neither the criteria for ex post evaluation nor approaches for measuring economic results are at all well developed. The development of consistent techniques for evaluating the effectiveness of public program performance on an ex post basis should be a high priority item on the research agenda of economists and other social scientists concerned with public policy. Indeed, it is now clear that

[1] See *The Analysis and Evaluation of Public Expenditures: The PPB System*, A compendium of papers prepared for the Subcommittee on Economy in Government of the Joint Economic Committee, 91 Cong., 1 sess. (1969), 3 vols. Many of these papers have been revised and expanded in Robert H. Haveman and Julius Margolis, *Public Expenditures and Policy Analysis* (Markham Publishing Co., 1970).

further extension of the application of ex ante economic analysis to public expenditure programs requires the demonstration that such analysis offers some prospect of isolating those programs and investments that would increase the net social return. Neither in the literature of public expenditure analysis nor in government practice should the efficacy of ex ante benefit-cost analysis continue to be accepted as a matter of a priori logic and faith.

The research effort reported in this volume deals with the ex post performance of a particular kind of public sector activity—real investment—and, within that category, focuses on public investments in the water resources area. It is an attempt to develop and apply an operational means of appraising the economic performance of public investments actually undertaken. Among the basic questions addressed in this volume are the following:

1. What conceptual basis is most appropriate for establishing a procedure for appraising the performance of public investments undertaken for resource allocation reasons (such as those in the water resources area)?[2]

2. What conceptual and empirical problems are likely to confront the analyst in undertaking the appraisal of completed investments?

3. What are some appropriate methods of empirically attacking the ex post evaluation problem—especially in the water resources area?

Although the scope of this study is not broad, the fundamental presumption on which it is based is of substantial importance: that real improvements in public sector performance will not be achieved unless information on the input (cost) and output (benefit) results of ongoing and completed government undertakings is incorporated into the decision process.[3] Indeed, because the behavior of decision makers in the public sector is influenced by a lack of incentives to achieve efficient programs, it is not unreasonable to presume that performance in this sector will not improve until the people themselves are informed of the results of ex post analysis.

Ex Ante Analysis and Ex Post Evaluation of Government Programs: The Setting

In 1965, when the Planning-Programming-Budgeting System (PPBS) was inaugurated in the federal government, the application of analysis and

[2] For elaboration of the basis for the assertion that public water resource activities are undertaken for resource allocation or economic efficiency reasons, see John V. Krutilla, "Efficiency Goals, Market Failure, and the Substitution of Public for Private Action," in *Analysis and Evaluation of Public Expenditures*, pp. 277–89.

[3] Charles Schultze has argued the need for ex post program appraisal as follows: "In many cases . . . our prior knowledge of production functions is quite limited. Uncertainty of this type puts a great premium on careful post-program evaluation. Feedback of operating results to program planning is essential." *The Politics and Economics of Public Spending* (Brookings Institution, 1968), p. 64.

quantitative estimation procedures to public sector programs was a mixed bag. In some areas, formal quantitative program analysis was nonexistent. In other areas, program analysis had been born but was an immature and fragile creature.[4] The application of analytical concepts to planning decisions was most advanced in certain of the public works programs and in national defense. The program with the longest tradition of formal analysis in the planning process was the water resources program. Since 1936, agencies responsible for water resources investments have been required by law to develop quantitative estimates of the benefits and costs of their undertakings prior to receiving congressional approval. Systematic analysis as a planning tool was introduced into the Pentagon under former Secretary of Defense Robert McNamara in the early 1960s.

In both the public works and national defense areas, program analysis is primarily of an ex ante sort. Confronted with a problem requiring public action (construction, expenditure, procurement), a decision maker expects analysis to yield a range of alternative options and an evaluation of the gains and costs of each and to isolate the most efficient or least costly among them.[5] In these ex ante analyses, relevant variables are projected to obtain estimates of the "demand" for outputs, and input-output relationships, which are at least partially known, are applied to obtain estimates of the supply of outputs and the costs of producing them. Many of the decisions in these areas are of an investment sort, and because such investments are characterized by heavy net costs in early periods and net benefits accruing rather automatically in later periods, the nature of the project (program) is set after the initial decision. This phenomenon has directed analysis toward the economic appraisal of alternatives prior to the investment decision.

Because of this emphasis on the initial decision and ex ante analysis in both the public works and defense programs, little attention has been paid to appraising the results of decisions already made or of projects (programs) that are in place and functioning. Such investments are viewed as past events, requiring no further decision. The need to evaluate the actual performance of the programs has not been sufficiently urgent to warrant the reallocation of scarce analytic talent from the task of ex ante appraisal to that of ex post evaluation. For this reason, little is known about the actual performance and efficiency of these undertakings, and still less is known about the relationship of experienced costs and benefits to their ex ante (or estimated) values. Little advantage has been taken of the potential feedback of operating results that could be utilized in the planning process. The seriousness of systematic biases in evaluation criteria and measure-

    [4] See *Analysis and Evaluation of Public Expenditures*, especially vols. 2 and 3.

    [5] In the water resources area, ex ante benefit-cost analysis is used more to evaluate unrelated project proposals according to a common set of ground rules than to evaluate the range of alternative actions designed to attain a particular objective.

ment procedures has not been appraised because of the failure to analyze the discrepancy between predicted and actual benefits (performance) and costs. Valuable information on the actual relationship of inputs (costs) to outputs has not been gathered when it was available.[6]

At the inception of PPBS in 1965, the role of analysis in the planning process of the social agencies was substantially more primitive than in the public works and defense areas. Quantitive and consistent application of either ex ante analysis or ex post evaluation was the rare exception rather than the rule in social planning.[7]

The failure of ex ante analysis to flourish in these programs is not difficult to understand. Because of the many economic and noneconomic objectives that provide the rationale for these social programs, there is no consistent methodology for applying ex ante evaluation techniques to the programs. The absence of an obvious and consistent methodology is reinforced by the pervasive lack of knowledge concerning input-output relationships pertinent to these social programs.

In fact, since the inauguration of PPBS, most of the analytical effort in the social areas has been ex post-type evaluation. Since there is neither a single accepted criterion nor firm knowledge of the relevant production functions, efforts to discover the kinds of changes that programs have produced and the extent of these changes are obviously of high priority. However, it should be noted that ex post evaluation in these areas does not occur against the backdrop of a prior ex ante evaluation. Here, the question is not one of eliminating the systematic biases of existing ex ante methodologies, nor is it one of refining knowledge of the parameters of input-output relationships. Rather, it is the very elemental question of gaining rudimentary knowledge of the production function and some insight into the substance of a consistent ex ante evaluation methodology.[8]

[6] It should be noted, however, that increased attention has recently been focused on both performance and cost appraisal and monitoring in the procurement of large weapons systems. These evaluation and control procedures are referred to as "performance measurement" and "should-cost analysis" and are conceived of as components of a comprehensive management control system. It is reported that efforts to develop and apply these efficiency tools have been resisted both by Department of Defense officials and by the defense contractors responsible for producing weapons systems meeting certain performance specifications. See testimony of A. Ernest Fitzgerald in *The Military Budget and National Economic Priorities*, Hearings before the Subcommittee on Economy in Government of the Joint Economic Committee, 91 Cong., 1 sess. (1969), pp. 595–617, 747–76, and 785–835, and testimony of Merton Tyrrell, ibid., pp. 495–519.

[7] See Joseph S. Wholey, "The Absence of Program Evaluation as an Obstacle to Effective Public Expenditure Policy: A Case Study of Child Health Care Programs," in *Analysis and Evaluation of Public Expenditures*, for a discussion of one of the first attempts in the federal government to apply ex ante analysis to the planning of a new social program. He states: "Generally, however, the federal government has made no real attempt to evaluate the effectiveness of its social programs."

[8] See testimony of Elmer B. Staats in *Guidelines for Estimating the Benefits of Public Expenditures*, Hearings before the Subcommittee on Economy in Government of the

The tendency for program evaluation in the social areas to be of an ex post variety is dictated in part by the relatively short period of time elapsing between the inception of the program and the opportunity to observe results. While some of these programs have long-run implications, they rarely have the long-term investment characteristics of public works undertakings. In most cases, the output will have been produced within a few years after the program expenditure. Indeed, many of these programs are viewed or should be viewed as basically demonstration or pilot efforts. As demonstrations, they can far more readily make use of the feedback results of ex post program evaluation in the process of program revision and budget allocation than can public works or defense investments.

It is worth emphasizing that the experimental character of social programs (in conjunction with the absence of prior ex ante analysis and input-output knowledge) has largely accounted for the methodological approach adopted in the ex post evaluation of these programs. While ex post evaluation and performance measurement of public works and defense undertakings have prior ex ante analysis as a bench mark against which actual program performance can be judged, there is no such yardstick in the social areas. For this reason, ex post evaluation of social programs has tended to be a matter of comparing the relevant observed characteristics of a selected group of people affected by a program with the characteristics of an analogue, or control, group of unaffected individuals. This difference between the nature of ex post evaluation in the social area and in public works (including defense) is a basic distinction that has not always been either recognized or appreciated.

Despite the time that has elapsed since the inauguration of PPBS, a substantial disparity exists between the social and public works investment sectors in the application of program evaluation techniques. In the public works budget (including defense), there is substantial ex ante analysis with little program monitoring or ex post evaluation, if any.[9] In most of the social programs, ex ante analysis is very rudimentary, input-output relationships are little known, and evaluative criteria are diverse and not unanimously agreed upon. On the other hand, the development of techniques for ex post evaluation of social programs has seen substantial progress in recent years and the potential for the feedback of ex post evaluation results into program revision is increasingly recognized.[10]

Joint Economic Committee, 91 Cong., 1 sess. (1969), pp. 3–96, for a discussion of the status of program evaluation efforts of federal social programs and the problem of evaluation in the multi-objective context of most of the social program areas.

[9] It is noteworthy that in the federal highway program there is little or no ex ante or ex post economic analysis of program investments.

[10] See Alice M. Rivlin, "The Planning, Programming, and Budgeting System in the Department of Health, Education and Welfare: Some Lessons from Experience," in *Analysis and Evaluation of Public Expenditures*, pp. 909–22.

OBSTACLES TO EX POST INVESTMENT EVALUATION

The research effort reported in this volume was stimulated by the failure of planning agencies in the public works area to gather and use feedback information from ex post analysis to refine and develop the ex ante evaluation model. The objective of the research is to explore some of the impediments to the application of ex post evaluation techniques, to suggest some operational approaches to the problem, and to apply these techniques to a few cases. In the water resource field, ex ante planning is in an advanced stage, but scarcely any attempt has been made to utilize feedback information. Therefore, the water resources program was chosen for this study in order to illustrate the problems, approaches, and techniques of ex post performance appraisal.

In this study, a widely held presumption is accepted—that the primary objective of public works investment is the provision of services that market failures prohibit the private sector from supplying adequately. Public sector responsibility, then, is to plan these developments so as to maximize net economic gain—the difference between social benefits and costs. This economic efficiency objective provides the analytical framework for this study. That is, the primary goal of ex post performance appraisal is taken to be the improvement of economic efficiency in planning for public provision of market-valued goods and services.[11]

Clearly, alternative objectives might have been chosen. The choice might have been to evaluate the entire range of impacts of project construction and operation—income redistribution, demographic change, regional development, and so on. However, given that the basic purpose of public works investment is to correct for market failure, it is judged that improvement in the methodology of estimating *primary* economic impacts should precede the ascertaining of a number of various and sundry nonmarket impacts. In addition, estimation of these nonefficiency impacts, even if possible, would require an enormous research effort. While outputs from water resource investment do influence the distribution of income, demographic patterns, and regional development, these changes are complex functions of an enormous number of variables, and not all the variables are project-related. Current knowledge and available statistical information are inadequate for filtering out the changes attributable to the particular public investment from the myriad other economic changes.[12]

Even though the range of program impacts evaluated in the study is re-

[11] The criterion adopted in this study is an economic, or resource allocation, criterion. It is not concerned with the financial feasibility of undertakings, nor is it concerned with whether or not the revenues generated by these undertakings cover their costs.

[12] On this point, see A. Myrick Freeman and Robert H. Haveman, "Benefit-Cost Analysis and Multiple Objectives: Current Issues in Water Resources Planning," *Water Resources Research*, vol. 6, no. 6 (December 1970), pp. 1533–39.

stricted to economic efficiency, several obstacles to meaningful ex post appraisal remain. Most of these are empirical or measurement problems, merely mentioned here but encountered directly in the empirical efforts that follow. These obstacles, it should be noted, apply generally to the ex post evaluation of all long-lived public investment undertakings.

First, if the primary purpose of evaluating the performance of existing public investments is to provide a feedback to the planner on the efficacy of his current procedures for ex ante project analysis, severe problems are caused by the evolution of agency evaluation practices. It does little good to tell the planner that his evaluation procedures of a decade ago were inaccurate if, in fact, significant changes in the process of project appraisal have been adopted during the intervening years. Given the evolution of evaluation methodology, it is necessary (1) to reevaluate the ex ante expected efficiency benefits of a project by using *current* evaluation methodology but data from the time of project construction, (2) to appraise the performance of the project from the date of project completion to the present, and (3) to compare the realized performance with the *reevaluated* prediction. Through this counsel of perfection, the analyst would have a description of the "state of the world" both at the time of the original ex ante analysis and at the time of the ex post evaluation.

If this procedure is to be used to develop an ex ante standard to which the ex post evaluation can relate, serious data and measurement problems are likely to be encountered. Appropriate data describing conditions at the time of project construction are not likely to be available in sufficient detail at a later date unless a deliberate effort has been made to preserve this information. For investments of the U.S. Army Corps of Engineers, for example, this effort has not been made for projects constructed prior to 1958 and only irregularly for projects constructed after 1958. To ascertain the values of the appropriate variables at the time of project construction requires an analysis equivalent in scope to that of an adequate project survey report. Consequently, accurate appraisal of existing ex ante evaluation techniques through ex post appraisal entails both the cost of reconstructing the conditions that prevailed prior to the undertaking and the cost of ascertaining current conditions for every investment to be studied.

A second obstacle is the "with-without versus before-after" problem. The basic economic efficiency criterion requires that the observed values of relevant output-related variables be compared with the values that *would have existed* if the project had not been undertaken. This criterion, it should be emphasized, is not the same as comparing the observed values of these variables with their value before the investment project was put in place. An ex post evaluation of this before-after sort is of no use to the planner in his efforts to improve evaluation procedures. If, for example, the flood losses actually prevented by a project were estimated and used as a basis for judging the benefits produced by the project, the appraisal of the project's worth would be greatly overstated. Implicitly, the appraisal would indicate that the prevention of damage to property induced into the floodplain by the project constituted a benefit attributable to the project. Such a claim has no economic rationale, because the additional capital placed on the floodplain would have been located on comparable land, which probably would have been flood free, if the project had not been constructed.[13] If ex post evaluation is to contribute helpful feedback to the planning process, it must avoid the simpler, more manageable before-after comparison and seek a measure of the difference between the value of flood losses that occurred with the project and flood losses that would have occurred if the project had not been constructed. It is not difficult to envision the added difficulties of a with-without appraisal.

A third difficulty encountered in developing a meaningful appraisal of project performance relates to the stochastic nature of some anticipated project outputs. For example, if a stream whose floodplain has been protected by a flood control installation demonstrates no flood-level discharge (under natural streamflow conditions) for ten years following the construction of the project, it is clearly not accurate to state that the value of the output of the project is zero. Rather, it must be recognized that the investment has afforded protection against the occurrence of a probabilistic event. It has, in effect, a value that is analogous to insurance. Consequently, evaluation of the real worth of the investment must account for the probabilistic nature of the hydrology of the stream. Substantial conceptual and empirical problems are involved in appraising the performance of investment projects whose output depends on such a stochastic process.

However, even though the realized benefits of a project depend on the actual hydrologic conditions that prevail in the river basin, it is not true that no meaningful results can be obtained by studying the natural streamflow pattern after the project has been constructed. At a minimum, the natural hydrologic record after the project has been put in place can shed light on either the quality of the ex ante hydrology study or the sufficiency of the number of years of record on which that study was based.

A fourth problem encountered in performing meaningful ex post analysis has to do with the nonmarket external impacts that accrue from nearly all public investments. If these impacts do not pass through an organized market, if they are not registered close to the site of project construction, if they involve nonmeasurable benefits or costs (or benefits and costs not commonly evaluated in monetary units), it is difficult for the analyst to distinguish the real from the pecuniary impacts and to appropriately account for the former of these values.

[13] In fact, flood damages to property that is uneconomically induced into the floodplain by the project are appropriately treated in an ex post analysis as "disbenefits," or costs attributable to the project.

A final obstacle to meaningful empirical evaluation of project perform-ance is the time pattern of the outputs of long-lived investments. For some investments, an analysis performed a decade following project completion may capture a significant portion of the total lifetime outputs of the project. For other projects, however, the time stream of expected outputs may dis-play a very slow start, with the bulk of expected project benefits occurring in the later years of the project's life. In the latter case, the analyst would find it most difficult to judge the efficiency of the investment on the basis of its output stream during the first decade. The appraisal of performance in this case is meaningful only after the lapse of a significant period of time after the construction of the project.

A Note on Prices and the Evaluation of Public Investments

As is well recognized, the outputs and inputs of private sector activities are automatically valued by the prices at which these goods and services are exchanged. Presuming competition, full employment, complete infor-mation and mobility, and the absence of externalities, these prices convey accurate evidence of the productivity of private sector investments. Prices enable the private entrepreneur to determine whether the returns from any of his investments exceed or are exceeded by the costs of the undertaking. They provide automatic feedback information on the ex ante investment analysis. This elaborate system of prices guides the economy toward an optimum level and composition of private investment.

For the public sector, however, this system of prices fails to provide feed-back information on investment performance. Plagued by the complica-tions of external effects and nonmarketable project outputs, public invest-ments often produce outputs that cannot be sold for a price. It is generally recognized that evaluation of the worth of investments producing such nonmarketable outputs must rely on more indirect evidence.

What is not often noted in the literature, however, is that even for public outputs that can be priced, there is often no pricing rule that can provide an accurate ex post appraisal of investment productivity or a guide to future investment decisions. Indeed, it is often implied that application of ap-propriate user fees to public project outputs would guide public investment decisions in the same way that market prices guide private decisions. Be-cause of the production characteristics of many public investments, how-ever, no pricing scheme exists, even in concept, to monitor the productivity of past investments or to guide future decisions. While claims have been made for the efficacy of both long- and short-run marginal-cost-pricing formulations and of the policy of pricing so as to recover full costs, neither provides accurate ex post appraisal of completed investments or guidance for investment planning. The basic reason for this result pertains to the phenomenon of increasing returns, which is common to investment activities of the public sector. In the face of this phenomenon, no pricing scheme can serve for the public sector the function that competitive pricing serves for the private.

Since Alfred Marshall, economists in the West have generally agreed that the prices of goods and services actually being produced should equal their marginal costs if an optimum allocation of resources is to be achieved. This proposition has been applied both to the outputs of firms in competitive industries and to those goods and services produced by decreasing-cost industries that require subsidization if production in the long run is to be maintained.

To be sure, when applied to competitive activities, the marginal-cost-pricing scheme does encourage short-run efficiency in resource allocation and does provide a sound guide for the expansion, contraction, or abandonment of fixed capital in the activity. Moreover, for such industries (and also for increasing-cost public enterprises), the relationship of costs and earnings under a marginal-cost-pricing regime provides an automatic basis for appraising the realized returns from, and the productivity of, completed investments.

However, for decreasing-cost activities, the evidence obtained by marginal cost pricing often fails to provide reliable guidance for matters of investment policy, whether the activity be in the private or public sector. As William Vickrey has stated: "It must be admitted that with decreasing-cost industries, a policy of marginal-cost pricing precludes the development of any . . . simple answer to questions as to which [investment] projects should be undertaken and which abandoned."[14] For these activities, the situation is as follows:

1. Prices that reflect short-run marginal costs insure optimal utilization of existing plant but, by themselves, provide limited guidance for the choice of future investment alternatives by these firms.

2. Prices that reflect long-run marginal costs may entail nonoptimal utilization of existing plant and, by themselves, give little basis for the evaluation of past undertakings.

3. Prices that recover full costs (over the long run) provide evidence for the evaluation of past decisions. Such prices, however, lead to underinvestment by encouraging decisions against those investments that demonstrate positive net benefits but that nevertheless cannot recover full costs.

While competent analysts can be found advocating each of these pricing schemes for publicly produced outputs that are marketable, most Western theorists have opted for some variant of the marginal-cost-pricing formula. Their choice, it should be noted, is primarily based on analysis in which

---

[14] "Some Objections to Marginal Cost Pricing," *Journal of Political Economy*, vol. 56 (June 1948), p. 218.

complete certainty is present and in which the optimal rate of output is the sole criterion. Conversely, a number of economists seeking policies and institutions for avowedly planned societies have claimed real benefits for the planning efficacy of full-cost pricing. These benefits stem from what has been referred to as "the sociological aspect of the marginalist principle"— the necessary tendency to "obligatory administrative interventions," "arbitrariness," and pressures for increased "bureaucratization."[15]

One could add to this the significant point that in a governmental and bureaucratic planning situation in which the vast majority of planning biases foster overinvestment, the suboptimal level of investment implied by the full-cost formulation may well be a salutary corrective.[16]

[15] Branko Horvat has stated the case for full-cost pricing as follows:

[With marginal cost pricing] there is no possibility to check the correctness of the estimate against the facts. There is, consequently, no possibility to correct mistakes while the plant is in operation. No fixed investment is absolutely fixed. Small changes, adaptations and additions to capacity are constantly being made, so that, if the full cost principle is applied, possible initial mistakes may largely be corrected . . . . If the estimates are not open to check, there is no possibility of improving the estimating procedures. All this seriously reduces the economic superiority of marginalist pricing over full cost pricing . . . .

One is, therefore, justified in concluding that, regarding the economic organization, the application of the marginal cost principle would be far from neutral. Inducement to substitute cost accounting manipulations for real improvement in efficiency, impossibility of checking the efficacy of investment decisions, administrative interventions in assessing the economic success or failure and obligatory administrative interventions in every act of fixed investment—all this spells arbitrariness and bureaucratization. The *productive* efficiency of an economic system varies in an inverse proportion with the degree of arbitrariness and bureaucratization it involves.

Accordingly, our final conclusion is definitely negative: the marginal cost principle is not desirable as a general pricing principle in planned economy. This does not mean that it is inapplicable in every single instance. For some specified cases, and in some special instances, it may provide a useful pricing or costing guide either in its pure form (e.g., toll-free bridges) or combined with the full cost principle as in two-part and multi-part pricing and price discrimination . . . .

We are, therefore, left with the choice of the second alternative, i.e., with the full cost principle. The analysis has shown that it is logically an imperfect principle but that, when applied, it is likely to lead to a better approximation to ideal output than the rival principle. This contention is based on the findings that, in the short-run, the full cost principle leads to approximately the same results as the marginal cost principle: with regard to investment, it is open to check and so immensely less arbitrary, and with respect to overall efficiency of the economic organization, it is superior. Even if *given* resources were better allocated on the marginal cost principle, the full cost principle would still be preferable.

For, when the *efficiency of allocation*—which is a static principle—*is compared with the efficiency of production*—which, in the sense of the growing social product, is a dynamic principle—the latter is preferable, *for it ultimately leads to a better satisfaction of human needs.* (*Toward a Theory of Planned Economy* [Belgrade: Yugoslav Institute of Economic Research, 1964], pp. 25, 27–28.)

[16] See Jerome W. Milliman, "Beneficiary Changes and Efficient Public Expenditure Decisions," in *Analysis and Evaluation of Public Expenditures*, pp. 291–318, for a discussion of further implications of alternative pricing schemes.

THE CONTENTS OF THIS STUDY

Improvements in the procedures for planning public investments and analyzing their efficiency require a regular feedback to decision makers (and to the public) on the performance of past undertakings. This feedback, it has been seen, cannot be provided by the comprehensive use of prices in the marketing of the outputs of public investments. Not only are many of these outputs nonmarketable, but, when increasing returns exist, there is no pricing scheme available to accurately appraise the performance of past investments or to guide future investments, even when pricing is possible.

Public sector planners, then, are thrown back on deliberate analytical studies of investment performance to guide their application of ex ante project analysis. While such ex post evaluation encounters serious obstacles, it is the only mechanism that can provide continuing feedback information on the efficacy of ex ante analysis and choice. Regrettably, this instrument of performance appraisal has yet to be seriously pursued by any federal agency responsible for public investment.

In part, the failure to apply ex post evaluation and monitoring systems to public investments stems from the lack of an operational framework for performance appraisal. Although the full development of such a framework will require a substantial research effort, the potential efficiency gains from the effort are likely to exceed the costs.

In the following chapters of this study, some of the basic problems encountered in any ex post evaluation effort are addressed, and a "first cut" at estimating some of the realized effects of public works investments in the water resources field is attempted.

Chapter 2 deals with public investments producing benefits in the form of flood damage reduction. After delineating the distinct outputs of such undertakings and defining the appropriate techniques for measuring the economic value of the benefits produced, possible approaches to ex post evaluation in this area are described and evaluated. Then, adopting what is referred to as the direct measurement procedure, a case study is undertaken to evaluate the ex ante analysis of the planning agency relative to the results of a particular project.

In chapter 3, much the same sort of approach is applied to public investments that provide waterway navigation facilities. After developing the economic concept of national efficiency benefits from waterway improvements, the existing procedures of the Corps of Engineers for ex ante evaluation are described, criticized, and illustrated. These procedures, it is concluded, measure values that have only a tangential relationship to national efficiency benefits and lead to benefit estimates that, on a priori grounds, are seriously overstated. This chapter concludes with an empirical ex post study of the Illinois Waterway.

In chapter 4, the energy output of a number of hydroelectric projects of the Corps of Engineers is analyzed, and this realized output is compared with the ex ante values of energy production as stated in preproject evaluation reports. The existence of systematic overstatement of expected outputs is found. This chapter also demonstrates that improved estimates of the value of energy output can be obtained by accounting for technological change in ex ante project evaluation. The monitoring of rates of technological improvement in power production and of changes in the length of life of steam generating facilities is required for the application of the proposed evaluation procedure.

The final chapter reports on the recent cost estimation experience of the civil works program of the Corps of Engineers. While this analysis demonstrates an enormous variance in the disparity between ex ante estimated and realized costs among individual projects, *aggregate ex ante program costs* conform rather closely to *aggregate realized costs*.

CHAPTER II

THE EX POST EVALUATION OF FLOOD
CONTROL INVESTMENTS

Chapter 1 indicated that the analyses of ex post evaluation reported in this study will focus on economic efficiency considerations. An inquiry is made into the value of outputs as defined by the model of standard welfare economics. Application of this model implies that each investment project or installation should be viewed as a production process—a process consuming inputs and producing outputs. This notion is essential for efficiency analysis because, typically, both the inputs and the outputs have a social value. The task of economic analysis is to determine if the value of the outputs produced by an undertaking exceeds the value of the inputs. Only if gains exceed costs is the undertaking judged efficient.[1]

The market system and efficiency analysis value both inputs and outputs in terms of dollars. As a result of the process of exchange, dollars become the common denominator that permits the comparison of otherwise incomparable items. Hence, the inputs to an investment project, when valued, become costs; project outputs, when valued, are referred to as social benefits. For each project purpose, then, the task of benefit estimation requires that (1) the nature of the output be defined, (2) the physical volume of this output be measured, and (3) a per unit price be attached to this output measurement. Similarly, inputs must be defined, their quantity measured, and a per unit value attached to them. This broad framework is used in the ex post evaluation in this chapter.

The chapter deals with public investments producing flood protection benefits. It is divided into three sections. In the first section, a discussion of the efficiency value of the outputs of flood control investments is presented. The second section is a description of two possible approaches for evaluating the efficiency performance of completed installations. Finally,

---

[1] This statement of the efficiency criterion is greatly oversimplified. For example, it ignores all constraints and noneconomic variables. For a more complete statement of the benefit-cost criterion, see A. R. Prest and R. Turvey, "Cost-Benefit Analysis: A Survey," *Economic Journal*, vol. 75 (December 1965).

an empirical exercise in the application of the direct measurement procedure for ex post evaluation is presented.

THE OUTPUTS OF FLOOD CONTROL PROJECTS

The following outputs of investments for flood protection can be distinguished: (1) the reduction of crop damage from flooding, (2) the reduction of property damage from flooding, (3) the reduction of noncrop output losses due to flooding, and (4) improvements in the productivity of land and property on the floodplain. Each of these output categories will be considered in the following sections.

The Reduction of Crop Damage from Flooding

Like any other output with economic value, reduction of crop damage from flooding has, in concept at least, a demand schedule associated with it. The demand curve derived from this schedule has a somewhat peculiar shape. It displays a rising portion for the initial units of flood protection service made available, followed by a downward sloping portion associated with output beyond some maximum incremental willingness-to-pay level.[2] A demand curve of this form is shown in figure 1. Given this demand func-

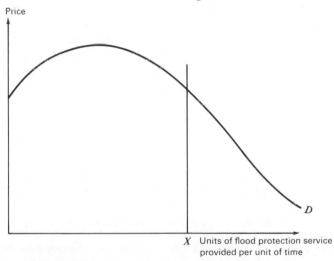

Figure 1. Demand function for flood protection services.

[2] This phenomenon occurs because of the pattern of floodplain development prior to the flood control project. Because little cropping takes place on that portion of the floodplain inundated annually or biannually, flood protection that eliminated only the one- or two-year flood would have little economic value. Elimination of the three-, four-, or ten-year floods, however, captures increasing amounts of willingness to pay per unit of flood protection service provided.

tion, the provision of a flood control facility providing an output level of X generates a total output value per unit of time represented by the area under the demand curve. If the demand function remains constant over time, the value of the output equals the sum of the areas under the demand curve for each time period, discounted appropriately so as to yield an estimate of the present value of the crop damages averted because of the project.[3]

The Reduction of Property Damage from Flooding

Here, as in the crop damage category, there exists a demand function for the output of the investment facility. Again, this function represents the willingness of beneficiaries to pay for the output per unit of time. The present value of benefits is indicated by the discounted sum of the areas under the demand curve for each year of the project's existence. Stated simply, the benefits in the form of property damage aversion equal the real cost of restoring property to its preflood value without the flood control installation less the cost of restoring property to its preflood value with the flood control project.[4]

In figure 2, the steps required to empirically estimate the present value of both crop and property damages averted are depicted and related sequentially to each other. These components of the empirical estimation process correspond to the method utilized by federal water resources agencies. As can be inferred from the figure, analyses of hydrologic conditions, forecasts of the physical performance of the installation, estimates of crop distribution patterns, seasonal planting patterns, flood-free crop yields and value components, and forecasts of "factors of increase"[5] *without the project* are essential components of the estimated annual benefits resulting from the reduction of flood damage to crops due to the flood control project. Similarly, estimation of the benefits of averting damage to property required estimates of stream hydrology, property values on the floodplain, project performance, and factors of increase *without the project.*

[3] If the demand function does not remain constant over time, the inter-temporal shifts in the shape and position of the function would reflect projected changes in cropping patterns that would occur in the floodplain if the project were *not* constructed and if no alternative means of flood protection were provided.

[4] It should be noted that the economic concept refers to the repair expenditures necessary to restore the property to its preflood *value* and not the cost necessary to restore the property to its preflood *physical condition*. The benefit estimate will be overstated if the cost of restoring the property to its preflood physical condition is the value estimated.

[5] "Factors of increase" are constants by which the estimated average annual damages at the present state of floodplain development are multiplied so as to yield the estimated average annual crop damage over the life of the project. These factors are developed from a regional base study that forecasts the growth of the region in which the project is located. Three things should be noted with respect to these factors and their application. First, by applying these factors by a straight multiplication procedure to estimated annual benefits at the time of project construction, it is implicitly assumed that all of the

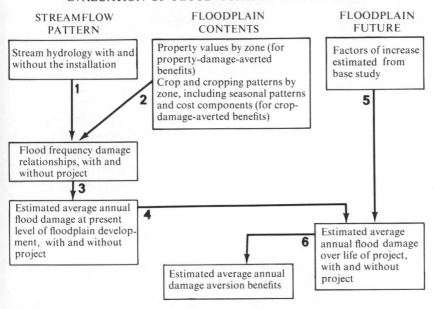

STREAMFLOW
PATTERN

FLOODPLAIN
CONTENTS

FLOODPLAIN
FUTURE

Stream hydrology with and without the installation

Property values by zone (for property-damage-averted benefits)
Crop and cropping patterns by zone, including seasonal patterns and cost components (for crop-damage-averted benefits)

Factors of increase estimated from base study

Flood frequency damage relationships, with and without project

Estimated average annual flood damage at present level of floodplain development, with and without project

Estimated average annual damage aversion benefits

Estimated average annual flood damage over life of project, with and without project

Figure 2. Framework for estimating flood control benefits.

The Reduction of Indirect Production Losses from Flooding

Within a smoothly functioning economy operating at full employment, there are several additional benefits from flood protection investments beyond those already discussed. While these benefits are not properly considered direct project outputs, a net willingness to pay for them does exist. These benefits result from a reduction of production losses associated with activities not experiencing direct physical damage from flooding.[6] Three illustrative situations are given below. In each case, the reason for the willingness to pay is different.

---

components of the damage estimate except crop yield (namely crop distribution, planting patterns, and components of crop value) remain constant over the life of the project. Second, because the factors are derived from the results of a compound growth pattern, the estimate of project life is crucial. The arbitrary movement from a 50-year basis of project evaluation to a 100-year basis has a far greater impact than simply extending benefit and cost streams by another 50 years. Finally, by applying factors derived from a regional base study, the agency implicitly assumes that the rate of development on the *unprotected* floodplain will equal the rate of growth in the entire base region. This assumption is both unverified and highly dubious.

It should also be noted that recent evaluation procedures of the Corps of Engineers have incorporated a projection methodology that is somewhat more refined than this crude percentage increase technique. For example, project analysis is now required to evaluate the growth of the floodplain in relation to the projected growth of the region, under the assumption of no flood protection investment.

[6] Losses of this type are becoming increasingly important. In the ex ante evaluation of many urban flood control projects, the benefits from averted losses of this form often exceed the estimated physical damage averted.

Case 1—A competitive firm with an essential input destroyed by a flood.

In many cases, indirect losses from flooding stem from the destruction of a crop that serves as the primary input for a processing firm. The direct flood loss is the value of the destroyed essential input. Other losses occur because the destruction of the input results in reduced output. If the firm is forced to restrict operations because of the destruction of its primary input, the social loss is the value of the output that labor, capital, and other productive factors employed by the firm could have produced had they not been removed from employment because of the restricted operation.[7] Additional social cost may result from (1) increased transportation for either factors of production or final goods, and (2) higher production costs in other firms if they increase their output in response to the reduction of supply from the affected firm.[8]

Case 2—A competitive business temporarily forced to reduce output because of flooding of facilities.

Social loss is present in this case because of the closing down of a production activity. Labor is temporarily laid off, and productive capital in place lies idle. As in case 1, the social loss equals the value of the output of the labor, capital, and other productive factors that are forced into idleness. If there is a long-term supply contract, production may not be reduced over the course of a period that exceeds that of the plant shutdown. Even in this case, however, there may be some social loss resulting from a less than optimum pattern of work imposed on employees because of disruption by the flood. In addition, the disruption of the stream of outputs from the firm may generate increased costs for customers.

Case 3—A competitive firm forced to reduce output because of flood-induced decrease in demand.

To the extent that labor and capital are forced into idleness (or into activities in which their productivity is reduced) because of a flood-induced decrease in demand on the floodplain, a social loss is incurred. However, if the business in question possesses alternative outlets, its output may not be interrupted. Sales not made to purchasers on the floodplain may be made to buyers elsewhere; in this case there would be no social cost, because no factors would be forced into idleness.[9] As in case 2, the presence of a supply

[7] If the productive factors are not forced into unemployment but are diverted into an alternative activity, the social losses are equal to the difference between their contribution to output in the first and second activities.

[8] This definition of indirect social loss holds except where other firms increase their output by hiring employees that either were laid off by the firm that shut down or were otherwise unemployed.

[9] This, however, sidesteps the question of the satisfaction of the alternative demands in the absence of a decrease in demand on the part of purchasers on the floodplain. If alternative demands could be satisfied even without the flood, then the occurrence of the flood does imply factor diversion somewhere in the economy and, hence, social loss.

contract would modify the results. Moreover, to the extent that demand on the floodplain is not destroyed but only shifted through time, losses in the form of increased inventory costs or losses related to the nonoptimum time distribution of consumption and factor employment are experienced.

Within this case, the special circumstance of perishable commodities[10] and services should be mentioned. To the extent that the reduction in demand implies lost and irrecoverable production, social losses are incurred. These losses are similar to those in case 1 and are represented by either the value of the perished commodities or the value forgone of the productive factors experiencing undesired idleness or diversion to less productive activities.

Improvements in Productivity of Land and Property on the Floodplain

One of the outputs of a public flood control investment may be an increase in the productivity of floodplain land because of the reduced incidence of flooding. For example, because of reduced flood incidence, an entrepreneur may find it profitable to shift floodplain land from low-net-yield pasture to high-net-yield agricultural commodities or to a factory site. In principle, this output is the net reduction in cost (or increase in net earnings) experienced by the occupants of the land because of the flood reduction services of the investment other than flood damage reduction.[11] In the water resource literature, the value of this physical output is known as "land enhancement benefits."

APPROACHES TO EX POST EFFICIENCY APPRAISAL

From the discussion of the types and social values of the outputs yielded by public investments for flood reduction, two approaches to the measurement of the value of realized outputs from such investments can be distinguished. These will be referred to as the *direct measurement procedure* and the *comparative land value procedure*.

The Direct Measurement Procedure

The direct measurement approach to ex post appraisal is a straightforward one. It requires a direct comparison of the values of the hydrologic, technologic, and economic variables that generated the ex ante project

[10] This refers to perishable commodities that are not physically damaged by the flood but nevertheless go unsold because of reduction of demand in the floodplain.

[11] A large number of cases can be distinguished in which the social value of the benefits from the increased productivity of locations on the floodplain would be greater or less than the value implied in this statement. However, the value implied in this statement is consistent with the assumptions normally employed in economic analysis. This problem is discussed later in this chapter.

evaluation with estimates of the realized value of these variables. Obviously, to implement this approach, the analyst must first construct or reconstruct ex ante estimates of the variables that determine project outputs, using data appropriate to the year of project construction. Then, he must estimate the value of these variables as they are actually experienced after the project is put in place. If this procedure is applied to benefit estimates themselves, the forecasted value of the primary economic benefits must be compared with the benefits actually experienced by those activities that would be present in the floodplain had the flood protection investment *not* been undertaken.

In implementing this procedure, the analyst either can rely on the ex ante estimation of project benefits (or the variables that determine benefits) developed by the public agency or can construct these estimates anew, using data of the period prior to project construction. If significant changes in ex ante evaluation procedures have occurred in the period since project construction, the analyst would be required to reestimate ex ante benefits and the variables that determine them, using the current estimation model. Only through such reestimation can the ex post evaluation provide a meaningful feedback to the planning process.[12]

In dealing with the economic variables that influence project benefits, the primary task of the analyst is to estimate the level and the composition of economic development that would have occurred on the floodplain *without* the installation. This estimation task pertains to the factors of increase that are applied to the data on activity levels present on the floodplain at the time of investment initiation. The objective is to derive an accurate estimate of the value of future damages expected without flood protection. Clearly, ex post, or realized, factors of increase representing actual growth on the floodplain in the absence of the investment are not observable.

A reasonable means of evaluating this economic variable would be to trace the pattern and rate of economic development in a region that is similar in economic structure to the project region, with the exception of project construction. The recorded factors of increase observed in this analogue region could then be taken as roughly applicable to the region in which the public investment is located. This procedure would establish a basis for estimating the pattern of development that would have taken place on the floodplain if the flood control investment had not been undertaken.

As an alternative to using an analogue region as a basis for estimating "without-project" development, one could assume that the project has significant economic impact only on the floodplain and not on the larger

<hr>

[12] See the discussion of the obstacles to ex post investment evaluation in chap. 1.

base region that encompasses the plain. On this basis, the analyst could estimate the without-project pattern of growth on the floodplain by applying the *observed* factors of increase of the base region. Here again, a region other than the floodplain serves as the basis for predicting the unobservable pattern of without-project floodplain development.

The crucial variable evaluated by either of these procedures is the schedule of factors of increase applied by the evaluating agency in the ex ante estimate of expected project benefits.[13] Implicit is the assumption that the hydrology study applied by the agency is accurate and that the variables, other than factors of increase shown in figures 2 and 3, are estimated accurately. Using a similar approach, the analyst could evaluate the ex ante hydrology study of the agency and the other variables essential to the ex ante estimate of direct benefits.

In estimating the realized benefits from *indirect* damage reduction, this direct measurement procedure must be modified. The first step required is the isolation of business firms that would have experienced losses from floods in the absence of the flood control facility. Then, these firms must be segregated into the categories consistent with the three cases of indirect benefits described earlier. For businesses in cases 1 and 2, the social loss of labor displacement due to flooding in any time period can be estimated by the total wages bill of the business in the time period just prior to the shutdown.[14] The social loss of forced capital idleness due to flooding in any time period can be estimated by the sum of time-related depreciation expense plus profit during the period in which the plant is shut down.[15] Case 3 can be treated in similar fashion.

Estimation of the realized benefits from increases in the productivity of floodplain locations, the final benefit category, presents the most serious measurement problems. In this case, the analyst must isolate the increment to, and the composition of, economic activity that would have taken place on the floodplain in the absence of the investment and must compare this value with the actual increment to, and the composition of, economic activity occurring on the floodplain due to increased real productivity of floodplain land. Through this procedure, the investment-induced productivity increase of floodplain land can be estimated. Stated alternatively, the analyst's task is to distinguish between (1) changes in the level and com-

[13] Further discussion of this direct measurement procedure is presented in the following section where an exploratory ex post analysis of an existing public investment with flood control as an objective is attempted.

[14] Implicit is the assumption that the labor is idle during the period of plant shutdown.

[15] Only the time-related portion of total depreciation expense during the period in which the capital is idle is a social cost attributable to the flooding. See the discussion of opportunity cost measurement under conditions of idle capacity in Robert H. Haveman and John V. Krutilla, *Unemployment, Idle Capacity, and the Evaluation of Public Expenditures* (Johns Hopkins Press for Resources for the Future, 1968), pp. 66–67.

position of economic activity on the floodplain attributable to productivity increases of floodplain land induced by the public investment, (2) changes in economic activity resulting from the natural growth of the area without the project, and (3) changes in floodplain economic activity attributable to inadequate or erroneous information about the extent of increased protection afforded the floodplain by the investment.[16] Having isolated that component of changed economic activity attributable to investment-induced increases in land productivity, the analyst must estimate the increase in the net earnings of these induced activities.[17]

Comparative Land Values as Indicators of Efficiency Performance

Under a highly constrained set of conditions, changes in the land value of locations within the floodplain will capture (1) the direct project benefits for crops and property damages averted, (2) the investment-induced productivity improvements (enhancement benefits) on land in the floodplain, and (3) the indirect primary benefits for cases 1 and 2. This set of highly restrictive conditions is as follows:

1. Markets throughout the economy are competitive and in long-run equilibrium, including the market for land in the floodplain. Buyers and sellers are rational and possess full knowledge.

2. Observed or implicit rents (capitalized into the value of the land) on all land in the floodplain equal the marginal value product of the land. This implies that increased rents are retained by the landowners who are flood control beneficiaries; i.e., the benefits of flood control must not be shifted and, hence, spread throughout the economy by, say, lower prices to consumers.

3. The rate of interest on which land purchasers make decisions equals the rate of return appropriate for analyzing decisions in the public sector.

4. Rents (and, hence, land values) observed prior to project construction capture only the marginal value product of the land at the time they are observed and include no anticipated returns from the construction of flood structures.

Presuming that these conditions hold, changes in land values will cap-

---

[16] See Gilbert F. White, *Choice of Adjustment to Floods* (University of Chicago Department of Geography, 1964) and Robert W. Kates, *Hazard and Choice Perception in Flood Plain Management* (University of Chicago Department of Geography, 1962).

[17] This estimate of realized benefits would accurately catch all the legitimate land enhancement benefits if the economy were in long-run competitive equilibrium, both at the time of project construction and at the time of efficiency performance appraisal. This position is consistent with that developed by Lind in his analysis of the estimation of social benefits due to increases in the productivity of land from flood control installations. See Robert C. Lind, "Flood Control Alternatives and the Economics of Flood Protection," *Water Resources Research*, vol. 3, no. 2 (Second Quarter, 1967), pp. 345–57; and "The Nature of Flood Control Benefits and the Economics of Flood Protection" (Institute in Engineering-Economic Systems, Stanford University, 1966, mimeographed), p. 88.

ture all the primary benefits of project construction with the exception of those referred to in case 3—output losses due to flood-induced demand reductions in the floodplain. To implement an ex post appraisal, then, a complete survey of land values both prior to project construction and at the time of the ex post evaluation is required. However, because changes in land values are caused by a large and complex set of economic forces in addition to the flood control investment, the observed increment to land values will typically overstate the benefits of the investment in flood control facilities. The observed increase, therefore, must be adjusted by removing from it those changes in land values that would have occurred without the project. This can be accomplished in some cases by use of an analogue region, such as the entire base region within which the floodplain is located.[18]

Appendix A contains a more formal discussion of the use of land value estimates in ex post evaluation and an evaluation of several of the empirical difficulties that plague this approach.

The John H. Kerr Reservoir—A Case Study in Ex Post Evaluation

The results of a pilot investigation into the realized effects of a flood control investment are summarized in this section. It should be emphasized that these results do not represent a comprehensive ex post analysis of the performance of this undertaking. Primarily, the results illustrate the kinds of problems confronted by, and the kinds of results expected from, ex post project analysis using the direct measurement procedure. In the analysis, an estimate of the value of realized benefits[19] from the investment will be compared with both the expected benefits forecast by the Corps of Engineers prior to project construction and the Corps estimate of project "benefits" in the form of actual flood damages averted.

The public investment studied here regulates the flow of the Roanoke River of Virginia and North Carolina, pictured in figure 3. Prior to its regulation, this river had a persistent, though not severe, flooding problem. The flooding was concentrated in the primarily rural areas of North Carolina covering the lowest 100 miles of the river's 400-mile journey to Albemarle Bay. The floodplain areas that experienced most of the damage lie

---

[18] The Corps of Engineers together with the Economic Research Service of the U.S. Department of Agriculture are investigating alternative procedures for discerning analogue regions using regional data in a multiple regression analysis.

[19] The benefits studied in this analysis are reduced flood damages to crops and property. Benefits from indirect production losses averted and the improvements in the productivity of land and property on the floodplain are not analyzed. For an empirical analysis of ex post land enhancement effects due to flood protection investments relative to the ex ante estimate of these effects, see Donald F. Theiler, "Effects of Flood Protection on Land Use in the Coon Creek, Wisconsin, Watershed," *Water Resources Research*, vol. 5, no. 6 (December 1969).

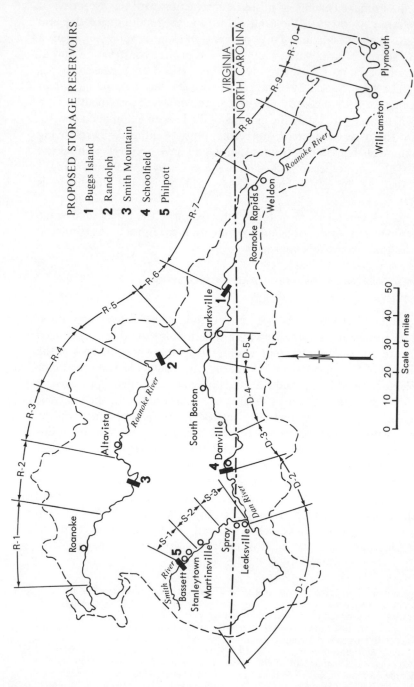

Figure 3. Damage zones in the Roanoke River basin. *Source:* U.S. Army, Corps of Engineers, *Report on Roanoke River* (1944), unpublished appendixes.

in regions R-7, R-8, R-9, and R-10 in figure 3. During August 1940, the river basin experienced a very severe flood. The crest of this flow was from 2 to 6 feet higher than previous floods of record on the river. Three lives were lost and several thousand people were made homeless. On the key gage at Weldon, N.C., a flood stage of 58.1 feet was observed. For the entire basin, a total loss of over $5 million was incurred.

Four years after that flood, the Corps of Engineers issued a survey report of the Roanoke River Basin based on a two-year study of the hydrologic characteristics of the river and the development potential of the basin.[20] It was concluded in this report that the level of expected flood damages failed to provide economic justification for the construction of a single-purpose flood control facility. However, according to the report, if hydroelectric power generation were included in the project design, a comprehensive river basin plan could be developed that would show a benefit-cost ratio in excess of unity.

Central to this comprehensive plan was the Buggs Island multiple-purpose project (later named the John H. Kerr Reservoir), to be located at the interface of regions R-6 and R-7 in figure 3. Designed primarily for the production of hydroelectric power, this project also was expected to yield significant flood control benefits. According to the Corps report: "It is estimated that the [John H. Kerr] project . . . would eliminate over 90 percent of the average annual flood losses in the lower part of the Roanoke River Valley."[21] Had the installation been in place in August 1940, the Corps estimated that over 70 percent of the experienced damages would have been avoided. For smaller streamflows, the installation would have eliminated an even higher proportion of expected damages. In the Corps report, the project was credited with $207,000 of annual flood control benefits in regions R-7 through R-10, given the 1940 level of prices and floodplain development then existing.

Ex Ante and Ex Post Estimates of Flood Damage

In this exercise in ex post evaluation, the impact of the project on flood damage in regions R-8, R-9, and R-10 of figure 3 is analyzed.[22] The functional relationships between streamflow, area inundated, and crop and

---

[20] U.S. Army, Corps of Engineers, *Report on Roanoke River*, H. Doc. 650, 78 Cong., 2 sess. (1944). Unless otherwise noted, all the data in this chapter are taken from this report or its unpublished appendixes, which were supplied by the Corps District Office at Wilmington, N.C. Although the report was issued in 1944, the data it contains is for 1940.

[21] Ibid., p. 81.

[22] Although region R-7 is below the John H. Kerr installation and, hence, a potential beneficiary of flood damage reduction, it is omitted from this analysis. Its elimination is necessitated by the construction of a private utility dam at the boundary of regions R-7 and R-8 shortly after the construction of the John H. Kerr project. This project resulted in inundation of the floodplain in R-7 and consequently eliminated the production of flood control benefits within this reach by the John H. Kerr project.

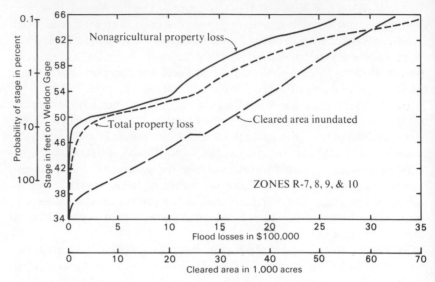

Figure 4. Flood loss and area inundated functions, Roanoke River basin. *Source:* U.S. Army, Corps of Engineers, *Report on Roanoke River* (1944), unpublished appendixes.

property loss due to flood damage as developed in the Corps report are accepted as accurate. These relationships, taken from appendix C to the Corps report, are shown in figures 4 and 5.[23]

From these relationships and data on the computed *natural* peak stages of the river at Weldon, N.C.,[24] the basis is established for estimating the flood damage that would have occurred had the investment not been undertaken. The data on natural peak stages extended from 1950, the first year of project operation, to January 1970. During this twenty-year span, the Roanoke River would have exceeded flood stage on seventy different days had the flow not been regulated—an average of 3.5 floods per year. For each occasion of flooding,[25] the stage-area inundated and stage-damage relationships were utilized to generate an estimate of the flood damage that would have occurred in regions R-8 through R-10 had the John H. Kerr

[23] It will be noted that the relationships in fig. 4 refer to regions R-7 through R-10. In performing the calculations necessary for the ex post evaluation, these functions were adjusted to eliminate the R-7 component. Data on the relationship of floods of varying sizes to damages in region R-7 in app. A to the Corps report served as the basis for this adjustment.

[24] These computed natural stage data show the levels the river would have attained had the project not been in place. They were obtained from the Corps of Engineers District Office in Wilmington, N.C.

[25] As mentioned earlier, no allowance is made for serial flooding. Hence, the ex post estimate of flood damage occurring without the project overstates the actual damage that would have occurred.

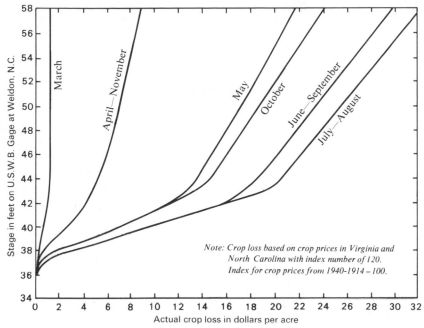

Figure 5. Crop loss functions for zones R-8, R-9, and R-10, Roanoke River basin.
  Source: U.S. Army, Corps of Engineers, *Report on Roanoke River* (1944),
  unpublished appendixes.

project *not* been in place and had floodplain development remained static
at the 1940 level. The conceptual steps in this calculation are shown in
panels 1 through 5 of figure 6. The estimated flood damage that would
have occurred without the project and with no natural development in the
floodplain is recorded in column 2 of table 1. Column 1 records the ex ante
estimate of damages for regions R-8 through R-10 as shown in the Corps
report—again, with no natural growth in the floodplain.

To estimate the value of flood damage that would have occurred under
projected floodplain development and property and crop value conditions
without the John H. Kerr installation, a set of factors projecting expected
natural growth was constructed for both the crop and property values. By
applying these factors, the value of flood damages to crops and property
is estimated on the basis of the development pattern that would likely have
occurred without the project.[26] This computation, shown conceptually in

[26] An annual rate of growth of 3.5 percent was applied to the 1940 crop damage
estimates. This rate is slightly in excess of the annual rate of growth in the total value of
agricultural output for the states of North Carolina and Virginia and for the five North
Carolina counties containing regions R-8 through R-10 for the years 1940 to 1965.
Implicit in the application of this rate are the assumptions that the development of
agricultural output that would have occurred on the floodplain of regions R-8 through
R-10 *without* the flood control project is equal to the rate of agricultural development in

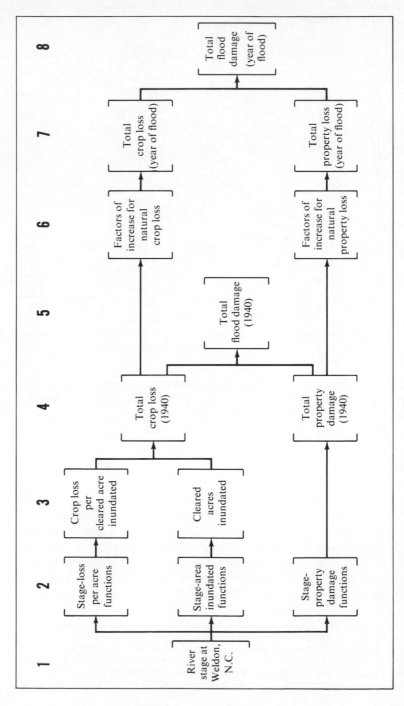

Figure 6. Framework for ex post evaluation of benefits, John H. Kerr Reservoir.

TABLE 1. Ex Ante and Ex Post Estimated Flood Damages without the John H. Kerr Project, with and without Natural Floodplain Development, 1950–1969

(*$ thousand*)

Year	With no natural flood-plain development		With projected natural floodplain development	
	Ex ante (1)	Ex post (2)	Ex ante (3)	Ex post (4)
1950	179.9	7.5	219.3	13.4
1951	179.9	24.4	223.6	45.8
1952	179.9	81.3	228.1	173.5
1953	179.9	17.9	232.8	37.7
1954	179.9	115.6	237.3	207.4
1955	179.9	291.8	242.1	519.6
1956	179.9	0.9	247.0	2.3
1957	179.9	40.5	251.9	107.5
1958	179.9	134.9	256.9	324.6
1959	179.9	2.6	262.1	8.0
1960	179.9	51.5	267.3	146.0
1961	179.9	26.8	272.7	90.2
1962	179.9	48.4	278.1	195.6
1963	179.9	39.3	283.7	134.7
1964	179.9	0.8	289.3	3.0
1965	179.9	7.4	295.2	31.9
1966	179.9	9.8	301.0	44.1
1967	179.9	0.8	307.1	3.6
1968	179.9	0.9	313.5	4.6
1969	179.9	1.1	319.9	5.5
Total	3,598.0	904.2	5,328.9	2,099.0

panels 6–8 of figure 6, produces an estimate of the flood loss that the natural streamflow would have produced in values reflecting expected development of the floodplain without the project. These ex post estimated flood damages without the project for natural (without-project) floodplain development are shown in column 4 of table 1.

Column 3 of table 1 presents the ex ante estimate of flood damages without the project for natural floodplain development. These values were derived by applying a 3 percent factor of increase to the 1940 Corps ex ante estimates shown in column 1. In the Corps report, no factors of increase were applied to the 1940 damage estimates.

As can be seen by comparing columns 1 and 2 and columns 3 and 4 of

the regions surrounding the floodplain and that agricultural development is uniform within the floodplain. This, in all likelihood, overstates the rate of growth that would have occurred in the absence of the project.

An annual rate of growth of 6 percent was applied to the 1940 property damage estimates. This rate is approximately the annual rate of growth of the gross income of the states of North Carolina and Virginia for the years 1940–65. Implicit in the application of this rate are the assumptions that increases in the value of real property are accurately estimated by changes in gross income, that the growth of real property values in the floodplain of regions R-8 through R-10 without the flood control project is equal to the rate of growth of real property in the regions surrounding the floodplain and that the development of real property is uniformly distributed over the floodplain. In all likelihood, this again overstates the without-project rate of growth.

table 1, the Corps ex ante estimates of the level of damages expected without flood protection are substantially greater than the level of damages that would have been experienced in the twenty years of project life. This is true on the basis of both no floodplain development and natural floodplain development. On the basis of no development, estimated ex post damages exceed the ex ante estimates of annual without-project damages in only one year of the twenty—1955. On the basis of natural floodplain development, actual damages would have exceeded expected damages in only two of the twenty years.

When the ex ante expected and ex post estimated damages on the basis of no floodplain development are summed over the twenty years, ex ante predicted damages are $3.6 million, while actual flood damages (estimated ex post) are only $0.9 million—a disparity of $2.7 million. The disparity between the ex ante predictions and ex post estimates is even greater when both values are adjusted for natural increases in floodplain development without flood protection. Using this basis, the sum of ex ante damage prediction over the twenty-year period exceeds ex post estimates by $3.2 million. It should be emphasized that these damage estimates refer to an unprotected floodplain.

Given that both the ex ante and ex post estimates are based on the same stage-damage and stage-area inundated functions, the observed divergence between columns 1 and 2 and columns 3 and 4 can be explained by some combination of the following: (1) an insufficient number of observations so that the extreme events of a correctly established hydrologic regime have not yet been manifest, or (2) an estimated hydrologic regime, accepted by the Corps at the time of the initial project study, that overstates the probability of very large streamflows. While investigation of the degree of divergence explained by each of these factors is beyond this study, evidence presented in the Corps report suggests that both factors contribute to the observed divergence.[27] The basis for this conclusion is summarized in tables 2 and 3.

Table 2 suggests that a longer period of post-project observation may yield a distribution of natural stage heights above those in the 1950–69 period. The data in the table show that, while 11 percent of the floods above the 35-foot stage exceeded 45 feet in the forty-one years from 1899 to 1940,

---

[27] The difficulty of attributing the divergence to one or another of these variables should be emphasized. The Corps made its 1940 hydrology study on a streamflow record of about forty years. The study could have been a poor one (even given the methodology available at that time) yielding an overstated projection of the distribution of streamflows. On the other hand, the forty-year record could have contained an unusually high number of very large floods that would have been translated into an excessive projection of flood frequencies. Finally, the years since the project began operating could have been years in which the natural streamflow was significantly below what one would expect from a correct ex ante estimate of the hydrology.

TABLE 2. PERCENTAGE DISTRIBUTION OF FLOODS ABOVE 35 FEET AT WELDON, N.C., GAGE, 1899–
1940, AND NATURAL FLOOD STAGES, 1950–1969

Period	Stage of stream (feet)			
	35–40	40–45	45–50	50 or more
1899–1940	63	27	9	2
1950–1969	79	21	0	0

Source: U.S. Army Corps of Engineers, unpublished app. C of Report on Roanoke River, H. Doc. 650, 78 Cong., 2 sess. (1944), and other data supplied by the Corps.

TABLE 3. ESTIMATED FLOOD FREQUENCY AT WELDON, N.C., GAGE

Probability of flood exceeding specified height in each year (percent)	Stage of stream (feet)
100.0	40.0
50.0	42.5
20.0	45.8
10.0	48.4
5.0	51.0
2.0	54.3
1.0	56.8
0.1	65.2

Source: U.S. Army Corps of Engineers, unpublished app. C. of Report on Roanoke River, H. Doc. 650, 78 Cong., 2 sess. (1944), and other data supplied by the Corps.

the largest calculated natural stream stage in the twenty years from 1950 to 1969 failed to exceed 45 feet.

Table 3 shows the ex ante hydrologic estimate of the average chance of floods of different heights occurring in a year. Although the Corps study showed a 100 percent probability of a flood of at least 40 feet occurring in a year, only 33 percent of the post-1950 years recorded a calculated natural flood stage of at least 40 feet. Although one would expect from the above distribution that ten of the twenty observed years would have experienced a flood in excess of 42.5 feet, only one year, 1955, witnessed a flood of that severity. It is reasonable to conclude that it is highly improbable that an observed twenty-year run would fall so far short of predictions yielded by an accurate hydrologic analysis.

Were such an extreme deviation of actual from predicted results to be consistent with an accurate hydrology estimate, prolonged drought conditions would likely have prevailed during the 1950–69 period. In fact, no such conditions were recorded. A comparison of rainfall records for Roanoke Valley show an average annual rainfall of 41.68 inches during the years after 1950 and an average annual rainfall of 42.10 inches over the fifty-one years from 1891 to 1941.[28] While the rainfall for the post-project

[28] It should be emphasized that comparisons of average rainfall are not, in themselves, sufficient to test the accuracy of a hydrologic estimate. Other parameters, including the intensity and distribution of rainfall, are also important determinants of runoff and streamflow.

period is lower than that for the previous period of record, the difference is not substantial. This evidence suggests that the Corps hydrology forecast contained a substantial bias toward large streamflows.

Ex Ante and Ex Post Estimates of Flood Control Benefits

In table 4, the flood control *benefits* expected from the John H. Kerr installation at the time of the Corps report (1944) are compared with the ex post estimates of realized flood control benefits. In the ex post calculation, the benefits credited to the project represent that portion of total estimated without-project damages (recorded in columns 2 and 4 of table 1) that would have been averted by the existence of the project. The first of these ex post benefit estimates assumes that the level of development on the floodplain remains static at the observed 1940 level. The second assumes that the floodplain developed at the rate expected *without* the presence of the project, that is, without incursion induced by flood control.[29] These ex post benefits are shown in columns 2 and 4 of table 4.

In estimating the ex ante expected benefits from the John H. Kerr Reservoir in areas R-8 through R-10, the damages expected with the project are subtracted from those expected if no flood control investment is undertaken. The former estimates are taken from the Corps report. The latter estimates, also taken from the report, are shown in columns 1 and 3 of table 1. The difference between the two estimates represents the ex ante expected flood control benefits attributed to the project by the Corps. These ex ante benefit estimates are shown in columns 1 and 3 of table 4, on the basis of no floodplain development and of natural floodplain development.

In columns 5 and 6 of table 4, the deviation of expected flood control benefits from ex post benefit estimates is shown for each year of the project's life on both of the assumptions concerning floodplain development.

Given the results of table 1, it is not surprising that the estimates of the realized economic benefits attributable to the project fall far short of the project benefit estimates presented in the Corps report. While total benefits over the twenty-year life of the project were expected to be nearly $3.3 million, assuming no floodplain development beyond that present in 1940, it is estimated that only $0.8 million of economic benefits have been generated by the project. This represents a shortfall of some $2.5 million over

---

[29] In estimating the realized economic benefits resulting from the John H. Kerr installation, the actual regulated streamflow pattern is played through the model described in fig. 1. The resulting damages are those that would have remained with the installation in place but with floodplain development reflecting without-project conditions. These damages are then subtracted from the damage figures in column 4 of table 1. It should again be noted that these estimates exclude the land enhancement benefits appropriately attributed to the projects.

TABLE 4. Ex Ante and Ex Post Estimates of Flood Control Benefits Attributed to the John H. Kerr Project, with and without Natural Floodplain Development, 1950–1969

($ thousand)

| Year | With no floodplain development | | With natural floodplain development | | Deviation of ex ante from ex post | |
	Ex ante (1)	Ex post (2)	Ex ante (3)	Ex post (4)	No development (5)	Natural development (6)
1950	164.6	7.5	200.6	13.4	−157.1	−187.2
1951	164.6	21.8	204.6	40.5	−142.8	−164.1
1952	164.6	80.4	208.7	171.5	−84.2	−37.2
1953	164.6	17.9	213.0	37.7	−146.7	−175.3
1954	164.6	109.4	217.1	193.4	−55.2	−23.7
1955	164.6	272.2	221.6	476.6	107.6	255.0
1956	164.6	0.9	226.0	2.3	−163.7	−223.7
1957	164.6	39.5	230.4	105.4	−125.1	−125.0
1958	164.6	118.3	235.0	277.3	−46.3	42.3
1959	164.6	2.6	239.8	8.0	−162.0	−231.8
1960	164.6	49.6	244.6	140.0	−115.0	−104.6
1961	164.6	25.5	249.5	85.8	−139.1	−163.7
1962	164.6	45.7	254.5	185.6	−118.9	−68.9
1963	164.6	35.2	259.6	119.1	−129.4	−140.5
1964	164.6	0.8	264.7	3.0	−163.8	−261.7
1965	164.6	7.4	270.1	31.9	−157.2	−238.2
1966	164.6	9.8	275.4	44.1	−154.8	−231.3
1967	164.6	0.8	281.0	3.6	−163.8	−277.4
1968	164.6	0.9	286.6	4.6	−163.7	−282.0
1969	164.6	1.1	296.3	5.5	−163.5	−290.8
Total	3,292.0	846.3	4,879.1	1,949.3	−2,444.7	−2,929.8

the twenty-year period, or an average shortfall of $125,000 per year. On the basis of no floodplain development, realized benefits exceed ex ante projected benefits in only one of the twenty years.

On the basis of natural floodplain development, the Corps report implied a total of $4.9 million of expected benefits attributable to the John H. Kerr project over the twenty-year period. In fact, only $1.9 million worth of benefits were realized—a shortfall of nearly $3 million. While ex ante average annual expected benefits were $244,000, only about $98,000 of benefits per year have been realized—an average shortfall of $146,000 per year. Realized benefits exceeded projected benefits in two of the twenty years on the basis of natural floodplain development.[30]

Ex Post Economic Benefits versus Actual Damages Averted

In addition to the comparison of realized benefits with projected benefits, another kind of comparison is of interest: the relationship of the appropriate estimate of benefits realized with the estimate of "benefits"

[30] In these computations, neither realized flood damages nor realized flood damages averted (benefits) were adjusted downward to allow for recorded natural flood stages that occurred within a short span of time.

TABLE 5. IMPACT OF THE ROANOKE RIVER FLOOD OF FEBRUARY 15, 1966, UNDER ALTERNATIVE
ASSUMED FLOODPLAIN DEVELOPMENT CONDITIONS, WITH NATURAL AND REGULATED
STREAMFLOWS

Item	Natural floodplain development	Actual floodplain development
Cultivated area inundated, natural flow (acres in R-8—R-10)	478	3,500
Cultivated area inundated, regulated flow (acres in R-8—R-10)	0	600
Total damage, year-of-flood basis, natural flow ($ thousand)	44.1	72.8
Total damage, year-of-flood basis, regulated flow ($ thousand)	0	8.7
Total benefits or damages averted ($ thousand)	44.1	64.1

realized with actual floodplain development, including damages averted
on that portion of the development that was induced by the existence of
the investment. Data for the flood of February 15, 1966, have been used to
illustrate the extent of floodplain invasion generated by the flood control
investment and the disparity between realized benefits estimated on the
basis of floodplain development without the project and Corps estimates
of actual damages averted. Table 5 summarizes some of the information
pertinent to this comparison.

The data in the first column (natural development of the floodplain
without the John H. Kerr installation) were calculated using the basic
model described in figure 6. The physical (stage-area inundated) and economic (stage-crop damage) relationships presented in the Corps study, together with Corps data on the natural and regulated river flows for the
period around February 15, 1966, formed the basis for the estimates of
cultivated acres inundated, ex post estimated damages, and economic
benefits.[31]

The information in the second column of table 5 describes the impact
of the flood with actual conditions of development. These data were calculated from the 1966 counterparts of the functions shown in panel 2 of
figure 6. Estimated by the Corps of Engineers, these functions enable calculation of cultivated acres inundated, damages, and damages averted with
both natural and regulated streamflows, given actual conditions of floodplain development, including development induced by the project.

The data of table 5 evidence a substantial disparity in the estimated impacts. On the basis of the updated 1940 stage-area inundated relationships
presented by the Corps, the first column shows that an *unregulated* flow

[31] The 1940 stage-damage functions presented in the Corps report were updated to 1966
to account for natural (without-project) floodplain development.

of the modest size experienced in February 1966 (34.8 feet at Weldon, N.C.) would have flooded about 500 cleared acres. However, given actual flood-plain development (part of which was induced by the project), the Corps estimated that 3,500 *cultivated* acres would have been inundated with an unregulated streamflow. With the Kerr project assumed to be in place, and with the streamflow regulated, it was predicted in the Corps report that a streamflow equal to that on February 15, 1966, would not have inundated any areas of the floodplain containing crops or property. On the other hand, with actual 1966 development conditions and a regulated stream-flow, it is estimated that 600 cultivated acres were inundated. This rep-resents more cultivated area than would have been flooded had the John H. Kerr project not been constructed, had the streamflow remained unregu-lated, and had floodplain development proceeded under without-project conditions.

The disparity in estimates of damages and damages averted between the two patterns of floodplain development is consistent with the data on area inundated. The damages that would have occurred with floodplain develop-ment consistent with no stream regulation are about 60 percent of the damages that would have occurred with unregulated streamflow and the actual 1966 level of floodplain development. With the streamflow regulated, actual damage amounted to nearly $9,000.[32] This is compared with an esti-mate of no flood damage at all with the project in place and floodplain development unaffected by the existence of the project.

The final entry in table 5 shows that the stream regulation services of the John H. Kerr project generated about $44,000 of economic benefits during the flood of February 1966 and averted flood damages of about $64,000.[33] The disparity between these two figures is accounted for by encroachment onto the floodplain because of the existence of the project. Only the first of the two figures represents real economic benefits attributable to the in-vestment undertaking.

Figure 7 presents some evidence on the proportion of actual floodplain development that is induced by the flood control project. There, three func-tions showing the relationship between the stage of the river and crop loss are shown for the months of July and August. The function on the left is taken from figure 5 and relates the dollar value of crop loss per acre to river level under 1940 floodplain development conditions. The intermediate function is the 1940 function adjusted to account for the level of floodplain development that would be anticipated in 1966 if the floodplain experienced

[32] Because at least some of this damage probably would not have occurred if the project had not been constructed, it is in a very real sense a cost to be attributed to the project in any comprehensive ex post benefit-cost analysis.
[33] It should again be emphasized that land enhancement benefits are excluded from the analysis.

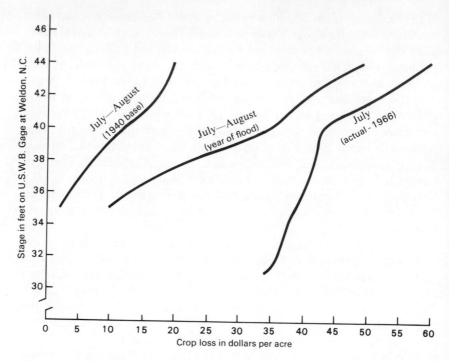

Figure 7. Natural flow crop loss functions for zones R-8, R-9, and R-10, Roanoke
River basin, 1940 and 1966. *Source:* U.S. Army, Corps of Engineers, *Report
on Roanoke River* (1944), unpublished appendixes, and data furnished by the
Corps.

the same rate of growth as surrounding areas—that is, if no project-induced
floodplain invasion occurred. The function on the right relates river level
to crop loss for actual 1966 floodplain development conditions.

Two characteristics of this diagram are of particular interest. First, for
any recorded stage, the actual damage per acre in 1966 is significantly
greater than that which would have occurred with natural (without-project)
floodplain development. That this difference appears on a per acre basis (in
addition to the significant increase in the number of cultivated acres inundated) indicates a substantial shift in the intensity and patterns of cropping in the floodplain. Second, the function for 1966 based on actual development begins at a lower stage reading than the function for 1940 and
that for 1966, assuming natural floodplain development. Because of regular
inundation, cropping was not undertaken in the immediate vicinity of the
river in 1940 and would not have been undertaken in 1966 had the project
not been built. Hence, bank overflows corresponding to stage readings
below 34–35 feet did not cause crop damage under these conditions. However, with streamflow regulation and the protection it offered, or was be-

lieved to have offered,[34] cropping apparently occurred far closer to the river banks. In 1966, a natural flow stage reading at Weldon, N.C., of 31 feet was regarded as an inundation causing crop loss.

CONCLUSIONS

While the results of this case study are based on a number of judgmental assumptions, they do demonstrate that the realized direct benefits of the project fell substantially short of the ex ante benefits estimate. An important determinant of this shortfall is a post-project natural streamflow record that contained a far lower frequency of flood level flows than would have been expected from the ex ante project report prepared by the Corps of Engineers.

[34] See White, *Choice of Adjustment to Floods*, and Kates, *Hazard and Choice Perception*.

CHAPTER III

THE EX POST EVALUATION OF NAVIGATION IMPROVEMENTS

Improvements in inland waterways, ports, and harbors, like other public investments, yield physical outputs of social value. And, as with other public investments, the real dollar value of the outputs and inputs determines the net worth of the investment. Navigation improvements are of value to society because they reduce the costs required to satisfy the demand for transportation services. The cost savings generated by navigation improvements are represented by the reduction in the value of resources that the nation devotes to the transportation of commodities and people.

In this chapter, the conceptual framework defining the economic outputs of navigation projects will be examined. Then, because of the unsatisfactory state of agency procedures for evaluating waterway benefits, the current practice of benefit estimation will be described and critiqued. This current practice will be illustrated by reference to a recent project report prepared by the Corps of Engineers. Third, the results of an empirical ex post performance evaluation study will be presented. Finally, some suggestions for further research pertinent to ex post evaluation of public navigation projects will be outlined.

NATIONAL RESOURCE SAVINGS FROM WATERWAY DEVELOPMENT

As with the output of flood protection facilities, one can envision a demand curve for the output of public navigation improvements. Possessing economic worth, the outputs of navigation improvements can be exchanged for dollars of income or for wealth possessed by some spending unit. That is, there exists a willingness to pay for these outputs. However, because of the peculiar set of institutions surrounding the transportation industry in the United States, the values to be attached to navigation improvement outputs fail to conform to any observed prices.

For example, although shippers utilizing the waterway would be willing to pay an amount equal to the savings in transportation expense they experience by using the waterway, this value, because of the institutional characteristics of this industry, will *not* represent the social value of the gain. To be sure, the savings experienced by the shippers utilizing the waterway would represent the real value of the waterway if the rate differentials that shippers experience equalled the real cost savings involved. However, while barge rates are presumed to accurately reflect the costs of the direct users of the waterways (bargelines), rail rates are generally conceded to be substantially above real rail costs. Hence, part of the saving experienced by shippers is simply an income transfer from the owners of railroads and/or the purchasers of their service. This portion of the savings to shippers, then, is a "pecuniary externality" and does not represent real savings of costs. While the willingness to pay to avoid property damage from flooding can readily be equated with the cost of restoring damaged property, there is no similarly ascertainable value in the case of the output of a navigation improvement.

To estimate the value of the net social benefits of a waterway improvement, then, we must seek to isolate the reductions in real cost and increases in transportation services due to the existence of the improved navigation facility. Figure 8 will be helpful in visualizing the meaning of efficiency benefits in this context. Assume that in a given region a volume of traffic (measured in ton-miles) is to be moved in a given period of time and that the real cost per unit of moving traffic is given by the curve labeled AC in figure 8. The height of the average cost function (AC) is determined by the technology of existing facilities in the year in question and the dollar value

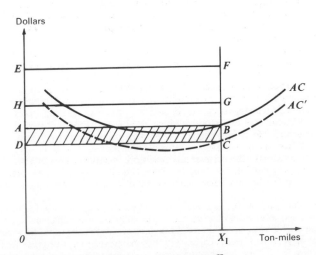

Figure 8. Price and cost relationships for waterway traffic.

of national resource inputs necessary to move the traffic.[1] The vertical distance is a weighted average of the unit costs of moving a given volume of traffic allocated by shippers among the various modes on the basis of effective rate and time-in-transit differentials. In computing the average, the unit cost of each mode is weighted by the volume of traffic moving on that mode.[2] For the movement signified by OX_1, the total value of resource (including congestion) cost is given by OX_1BA.

Assuming that the volume of ton-miles to be moved is fixed at OX_1 (i.e., a completely inelastic demand function), the efficiency impact of any improvement in transportation facilities will be reflected in the height of the average cost function. Thus, if the incremental cost of movement by water is less than the unit cost of an alternative mode, and if this differential is reflected in lower charges (adjusted for delay time) to shippers on water relative to the alternative, the creation of a waterway capable of transporting barge traffic will reduce the observed level of the average cost function.[3] The construction and use of the new facility will result in a downward shift in AC function to, say, AC' with the size of the shift being a function of the decrease in the unit costs of transportation on the waterway and the amount of traffic that shifts to the waterway from an alternative mode. Given that OX_1 units of traffic must be carried, the shift in AC shown in

[1] The resource costs included in the AC function include both the "straight-through operating" costs of transportation provision plus the "delay-time" (or congestion) costs. If for no other reason, it is this latter component of costs that causes the average cost function to rise. See Charles W. Howe and others, "Optimum Traffic Flow, Congestion, and Design in a Waterway System: Determination by Simulation," in *Inland Waterway Transportation: Studies in Public and Private Management and Investment Decisions* (Resources for the Future, 1969).

[2] Hence, the average cost function displays unit costs after each shipper has chosen the least expensive mode of transportation as reflected in the rates he faces. It should be noted that the AC function is not the least-cost function for moving OX_1 units of traffic. Because of the disparity in the extent to which rates exceed costs among modes, some shipments may be moving on a high-cost alternative when average costs are estimated. Indeed, because of this disparity, the public improvement of a waterway may cause some traffic to shift to the higher-cost improved waterway from a lower-cost alternative.

[3] The new average cost function will again reflect real costs after shippers have allocated their commodities among the alternative modes. Thus, if no shipper decides to use the newly created facilities (because of, say, monopolistic pricing practices or other market imperfections), the observed average cost curve will not shift down at all because of the improvement. Or, if the reduced barge rates on the improved facility cause some traffic to shift from a lower-cost alternative to the higher-cost waterway, the observed average cost curve may rise because of the improvement. Consequently, the national resource savings depend on both the volume of traffic using the new facility and the resource cost that would have been incurred in moving that traffic without the improved facility.

Moreover, the effect on the average cost of the alternative modes due to diversion of traffic *to the waterway* must be entered in the calculation of the new AC curve. For example, one could conceive of the opening of a new waterway diverting traffic from a railroad that already had excess capacity, thus raising the incremental costs of railroad transportation. The net impact of reduced costs on the traffic using the new facility and increased costs on the traffic remaining on the old facility might conceivably balance in such a case, leaving no *net* gain.

figure 8 implies that the total value of annual resource cost decreases from OX_1AB to OX_1CD, resulting in a total annual resource cost saving of $DCBA$.[4]

By assuming that the demand curve for ton-miles of highly substitutable transportation services is completely inelastic, a major component of the real value of investments in waterway facilities has been neglected. In reality, if the provision of waterway services results in a lower-priced alternative transport mode, the number of units of transportation service demanded will likely increase.[5] This effect, which is attributable to the waterway, must also be included in the benefit estimate. The analysis of this component of benefits attributable to the public investment is shown in figure 9.

Assume that, before the waterway improvement, the average effective rate[6] was OE and that OX_1 units of transportation services were being purchased. Assume also that the impact of the improved waterway was to generate a reduction in the average effective rate from OE to OH and that this lower rate yielded an increase in traffic from OX_1 to OX_2. The shaded area X_1FIX_2 then represents a gross value generated by the existence of the waterway. This value less the incremental cost of moving the traffic increment $[OX_2\text{-}OX_1]$ measures the net value of the additional transportation services and must be included in the benefit estimate.[7] The increment to

[4] It should be emphasized again that the savings to shippers may substantially exceed the national resource saving resulting from the provision of a new lower-cost facility. For example, in the realistic case in which railroad rates are administratively set significantly above incremental rail costs, while barge rates more closely approximate barge costs, the savings to shippers who shift from rail to water transportation would substantially exceed the savings in costs. In terms of fig. 8, a hypothesized decrease in the weighted average effective rate from OE to OH would exceed the decrease in unit costs. Thus, while the value of annual resource saving was $DCBA$, the annual saving to shippers would be the larger rectangle $EFGH$. Similarly, this estimated saving in resource costs attributable to the waterway will likely exceed the cost savings that would be realized if the OX_1 units of traffic moved on the least-cost mode both before and after the waterway improvement.

[5] This increase in the quantity demanded from a lower-priced mode is the sum of a direct and an indirect effect. The direct effect is the increment to traffic from lower barge rates, which are a direct result of the investment. The indirect effect is the traffic increase from railroad rates, which are reduced toward costs by the presence of waterway competition. Given that regulatory agencies would fail to reduce railroad rates toward costs in the absence of the waterway, it is reasonable to attribute both of the impacts to the waterway.

[6] The average effective rate is a weighted average of prevailing rates for transportation services, using the volume (ton-miles) of traffic using each mode as weights. The reduction of the average effective rate, then, is due to both the direct and indirect impacts as discussed in the previous footnote.

[7] See Howe and others, "Optimum Traffic Flow," for a discussion of the economic benefits from newly generated traffic. As they point out, the cost saving on existing traffic may understate or overstate the true benefits depending on the institutional conditions determining use of the waterway. In the analysis presented in the text, total traffic and its allocation among modes is taken to be a function of observed rates only. Depending on the level of observed rate structures, then, the total volume of traffic may or may not be the social optimum.

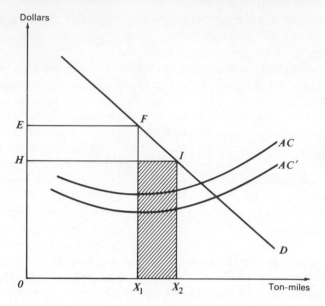

Figure 9. Demand and cost relationships for waterway traffic.

cost, it should be noted, is the sum of the incremental costs of the newly generated traffic, whether the traffic is carried by water or an alternative mode.

The *total* willingness to pay for the navigation improvement is equal to the sum of the reduction in costs of moving existing traffic (*DCBA*, in figure 8) and the *net* willingness to pay for the additional traffic generated by the improvement (X_1FIX_2 less the sum of incremental costs of moving $[OX_2\text{-}OX_1]$ in figure 9). This sum represents the total value of economic efficiency benefits attributable to the waterway investment.

THE COMPONENTS OF NAVIGATION BENEFITS AND THEIR EX ANTE MEASUREMENT

In the conceptual discussion in the preceding section, it was concluded that the benefits of investments in navigation improvements equal the unit reduction in cost for moving existing traffic plus the excess of the willingness of transportation service demanders to pay for additional units of transportation over the marginal cost of supplying them. Although this conceptual framework can be applied to transportation improvements in general, it is of particular use in discussing the procedures for performing ex ante empirical evaluation of individual navigation projects.

In terms of the preceding discussion, the components of the real value of benefits from an investment in navigation facilities are as follows:

1. Reduction in real transportation costs on those units of existing traffic that already use the waterway.

2. Reduction in real transportation costs on those units of existing traffic that shift from alternative transportation modes to the waterway.[8]

3. The net change in real transportation costs on those units of existing traffic that remain on alternative transportation modes.[9]

4. The willingness to pay (relevant area under the demand curve of figure 9) for additional transportation services by purchasers entering any transport market (i.e., rail, highway, waterway) because of the reduced average effective rate resulting from the waterway improvement less the marginal cost of supplying these additional services.[10]

In undertaking the empirical estimation of the total expected benefits of a proposed navigation improvement, each of these components must be specifically evaluated. The following procedure is derived from the above analysis; its application would yield a close approximation to the real social value of project-generated benefits:

1. The traffic that will use the waterway after its improvement will be of three kinds:

(a) Traffic that shifts to the waterway from alternative modes because of rate differentials (adjusted for time-in-transit differentials). To estimate the traffic in this category, the analyst has to estimate the response of traffic to rate and time-in-transit differentials.[11] Assuming that units of transportation service are homogeneous, this estimate for any given year can be based on the following functional statement:

$$T_n^w = F (R_n^a - R_n^w)$$

where

T_n^w = the traffic on the waterway in year n from the shift phenomenon,
R_n^a = the rate charged on the alternative mode in year n,
R_n^w = the rate on the waterway in year n.

Total traffic over the life of the project generated by this shift is $\sum T_n^w$ over the x years of the project. The important thing to note about this procedure

---

[8] There is a basic analytic problem involved in estimating the real cost savings on units of traffic shifting to the improved waterway because of the institutions surrounding the setting of rates for regulated transportation. Because regulated rail rates may remain above incremental rail costs after construction of the waterway, units of traffic may be induced to shift from lower real cost movement by rail to higher real cost movement by water. The cost saving on such shifts is negative. This problem is discussed further later in this chapter.

[9] This saving may reflect a reduction in congestion costs associated with use of the alternative modes prior to waterway improvement and the concomitant traffic shift.

[10] Estimation of this value for individual projects is empirically difficult. For example, how does one separate the additional traffic generated by the waterway improvement from traffic shifts from other regional transportation markets attributable to the intrusion of a new source of supply?

[11] This, in turn, implies the estimation of the relationship between rate changes and cost changes on alternative transport modes.

is that the estimate of traffic in future years must be related to the *rate differentials*[12] projected for future years.

(b) Traffic that will move on the waterway even with no improvement. For traffic of this type, the analyst must project the growth of both sources of traffic that now utilize the waterway and new sources of traffic that will be water oriented by nature of their product.

(c) New traffic generated by the improvement. For this traffic the analyst must estimate the elasticity of demand for new waterway transportation, forecast future barge rates, and, on the basis of these estimates, calculate the volume of new traffic on the waterway that will be generated by the reduced barge rates.[13]

2. Presuming that the waterway improvement is undertaken, the national cost savings on traffic of type (a) and that part of (b) that would have moved without the navigation improvement will equal the sum of the incremental costs on alternative modes of transportation less the sum of the incremental costs of transportation on the waterway (including differentials in handling costs). In the case of traffic of type (b), the alternative mode of transportation is the undeveloped river. For the remainder of traffic (b)—new sources of water-oriented traffic—and traffic of type (c), the benefit equals the willingness of the demanders of the service of the waterway to pay for it (i.e., the area under the demand curve for the generated waterway traffic) less the marginal cost of supplying the service.

3. The willingness to pay for the additional nonwaterway traffic generated by the reduced rates on alternative modes, less the sum of marginal cost of moving this traffic, must also be credited as benefits to the waterway improvement if it is assumed that rates on alternative modes that prevail before the waterway improvement are artificially maintained at an arbitrarily high level; that the public sector is constrained from affecting the height of the rates through direct regulation; and that the competition generated by the waterway will effect a reduction in the rates on alternative modes.[14]

In figures 10–13, the procedural steps required for accurate empirical estimation of each of these components of total navigation benefits are shown.[15]

[12] It should be noted that any differences in shippers' costs associated with alternative modes, such as handling charges, are included in the "rate differentials" concept used here.

[13] The analyst must take care to distinguish the elasticity of demand for newly generated traffic from the elasticity of demand for traffic shifting from alternative modes. The latter is treated under traffic type (a) above.

[14] These assumptions were made in the analysis of fig. 9.

[15] In addition to these benefits from traffic that would move by alternative means in the absence of the waterway, existing Corps procedures recognize a number of benefit sources from waterway improvement. Among them are the following:
a. Removal of hazards to shipping.

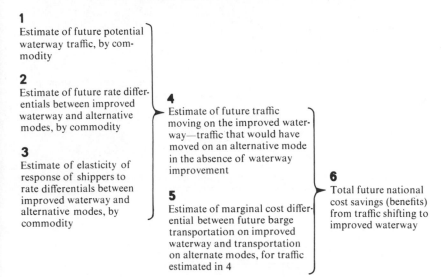

1
Estimate of future potential waterway traffic, by commodity

2
Estimate of future rate differentials between improved waterway and alternative modes, by commodity

3
Estimate of elasticity of response of shippers to rate differentials between improved waterway and alternative modes, by commodity

4
Estimate of future traffic moving on the improved waterway—traffic that would have moved on an alternative mode in the absence of waterway improvement

5
Estimate of marginal cost differential between future barge transportation on improved waterway and transportation on alternate modes, for traffic estimated in 4

6
Total future national cost savings (benefits) from traffic shifting to improved waterway

Figure 10. Estimation of navigation benefits on commodities shifting from alternative modes to the waterway.

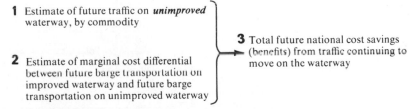

1 Estimate of future traffic on *unimproved* waterway, by commodity

2 Estimate of marginal cost differential between future barge transportation on improved waterway and future barge transportation on unimproved waterway

3 Total future national cost savings (benefits) from traffic continuing to move on the waterway

Figure 11. Estimation of navigation benefits on commodities that would be shipped on the unimproved waterway.

THE CURRENT PRACTICE OF EX ANTE NAVIGATION BENEFIT ESTIMATION

Current agency practice in the ex ante estimation of navigation benefits has been determined by direct congressional action in the Department of Transportation Act of 1966. This is the only category of benefits for which Congress has explicitly dictated the definition of benefits and the concepts to be used by agencies in evaluation efforts. Largely because of this inter-

---

    b. Benefits to commercial and sport fishing and recreational boating activities from elimination of delays in entering and leaving a harbor, reduction in spoilage of fish, and reduction in loss of, or damage to, vessels and gear.

    c. Land enhancement due to navigation projects.

    In addition to these benefits, there also may be adverse effects on overland transportation because of the costs of providing greater clearances for bridges, increased operation and maintenance costs of bridges, and so on.

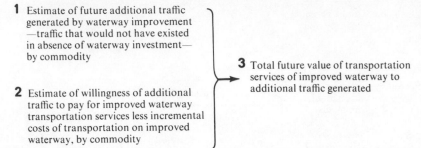

1 Estimate of future additional traffic generated by waterway improvement —traffic that would not have existed in absence of waterway investment— by commodity

2 Estimate of willingness of additional traffic to pay for improved waterway transportation services less incremental costs of transportation on improved waterway, by commodity

3 Total future value of transportation services of improved waterway to additional traffic generated

Figure 12. Estimation of navigation benefits from additional traffic generated by barge-rate reductions induced by waterway improvement.

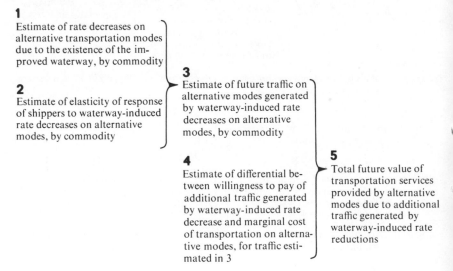

1
Estimate of rate decreases on alternative transportation modes due to the existence of the improved waterway, by commodity

2
Estimate of elasticity of response of shippers to waterway-induced rate decreases on alternative modes, by commodity

3
Estimate of future traffic on alternative modes generated by waterway-induced rate decreases on alternative modes, by commodity

4
Estimate of differential between willingness to pay of additional traffic generated by waterway-induced rate decrease and marginal cost of transportation on alternative modes, for traffic estimated in 3

5
Total future value of transportation services provided by alternative modes due to additional traffic generated by waterway-induced rate reductions

Figure 13. Estimation of navigation benefits from additional traffic generated by reductions in non-barge transportation rates induced by waterway improvement.

vention, current navigation evaluation procedures deviate more from ideal procedures than in any other project purpose. Indeed, most professional economists familiar with this area judge that existing congressionally imposed standards foster overinvestment in navigation facilities and inefficiency in the choice among alternatives. In this section, the recent evaluation of Corps benefit estimation practice will be described, and the serious inefficiencies fostered by the legislative directive will be pointed out.[16]

---

[16] See James R. Nelson, "Policy Analysis in Transportation Programs," in *The Analysis and Evaluation of Public Expenditures: The PPB System*, A compendium of papers prepared for the Subcommittee on Economy in Government of the Joint Economic Committee, 91 Cong., 1 sess. (1969), pp. 1102–27.

The waterway benefit evaluation procedures utilized by the Corps of Engineers prior to 1960 have been described by Otto Eckstein.[17] Pre-1960 Corps practice was to evaluate the *unit* benefits of a navigation improvement by comparing the current rates that shippers would pay to transport commodities on the improved waterway with the rates they would pay for the next best alternative mode. Eckstein demonstrates that, because of the complex nature of the railroad rate-making process and the setting of railroad rates to cover full costs, it is the unit *savings to shippers* that are being estimated and not national resource cost savings per unit of traffic moved. He states:

> The benefits of navigation, as measured currently by the Corps of Engineers, therefore, substantially overstate the saving of cost realized by the nation as a whole.[18]

In estimating the volume of traffic that would utilize a proposed waterway, the Corps employed a survey of the commerce flowing into and out of the region.[19] On the basis of the surveys, an estimate was made of the volume of future traffic that would move by water. In practice, a sizable share of expected traffic growth in the region was often credited to the construction of the waterway and projected as waterway traffic. For commodities that already moved (at least partially) on the waterway, the volume of traffic expected to shift from alternative modes to the waterway was judgmentally projected on the basis of a comparison of the freight charges on and off the waterway, using current alternative-mode rates and barge rates expected to prevail upon completion of the waterway.[20]

In this procedure, it was implicitly assumed that the difference between rail rates and barge rates would not change during the life of the project, either because of technological change in the railroad or barge industries or because of the competition of the waterway. Because post-waterway railroad rates are likely to decrease below their preproject counterparts by more than barge rates for both of these reasons, there is sound a priori reason to expect that the traffic projected on the waterway by this technique is overstated. Prior to 1960, then, the procedures used to estimate both traffic on the waterway and unit savings on this traffic led to bloated estimates of the benefits from navigation improvements.

In 1960, a significant change in procedure was adopted by the Corps.

[17] Otto Eckstein, *Water Resource Development: The Economics of Project Evaluation* (Harvard University Press, 1958).

[18] Ibid., p. 174.

[19] See the testimony of James R. Nelson concerning this survey technique, in *Economic Analysis and the Efficiency of Government*, Hearings before the Subcommittee on Economy in Government of the Joint Economic Committee, 91 Cong., 1 sess. (1969), pp. 489–90.

[20] These rates were calculated on the assumption that barge lines would establish rates that would cover full costs.

The use of transportation rates was dropped, at least in concept, in favor of a comparison of the resource costs of shipping commodities by water with the costs of transporting them by an alternative mode in the absence of the project. The change, however, still permitted rates to be used as an estimate of railroad costs when estimates of railroad costs were unavailable. In practice, the use of rates became the rule.[21]

However, even after the 1960 change, estimates of traffic expected to move on the waterway remained based on a comparison of *current* rail rates[22] and barge rates expected to prevail when the waterway is completed.[23] This is so even though the possibility of dramatic decreases in railroad rates—compelled by the competition of the improved waterway—was noted in a Corps engineering manual.[24]

The following quotations from the Corps manual summarize the benefit measurement procedure after the 1960 change:

> The costs of movement of commodities by alternative means may not be as readily available as are the rates published by carriers for such movements. Such rates may or may not reflect actual costs involved. Thus, analysis of transportation savings based on such rates may not give a true measure of the value of a waterway improvement. Where it is not possible to obtain actual cost figures for movement by alternative means, published rates may be used when, in the opinion of reporting officers, they fairly represent costs. Where there is strong possibility that the rates for movements under consideration do not approximate costs, the best estimates of overland carrier costs will be used in the analysis. Thus, in any case where rates are used as a basis for computing the cost of movement by alternative means, the relationship of rates to costs must be established. In making a decision in such cases whether to use available rates or attempt to secure costs, the principle should be followed that precision and refinement of estimates should not exceed the degree required to reach a sound judgment as to project justification.
>
> While comparative costs determine the economic justification of a waterway improvement, rates may have an important effect on the economic analysis because the actual level of rates will determine whether traffic will move on the waterway. A drastic reduction in overland rates might be sufficient to prevent movements of commodities by water, even though such action would not be justified from the broad public viewpoint. Studies of potential waterway traffic should, therefore, recognize the possible impact of varying rate levels and include an analysis of the effect upon projected use of the waterway of significant deviations in rates from cost levels.

[21] In some cases, however, this revision enabled the lowest observed rail rates to be used in project evaluation.

[22] In some cases, the lowest observed rail rates were used.

[23] This 1960 change incorporates the suggested procedures outlined in "The Green Book." See Federal Inter-Agency River Basin Committee, Subcommittee on Benefits and Costs, *Proposed Practices for Economic Analysis of River Basin Projects* (1950).

[24] U.S. Army, Corps of Engineers, "Engineering Manual for Civil Works" (mimeographed).

Consequently, while the new cost-based procedures were superior in concept to pre–1960 procedures, in practice the reported estimates were similar under both methods. Because of insufficient comparative cost data or insufficient understanding of patterns of rail rates after waterway construction, the use of current rates to estimate both traffic and unit savings remained the standard procedure for analysts in the field.

In October 1964, however, a second revision in evaluation procedures was announced. This alteration—which took the form of an interim procedure to replace the post–1960 cost-basis-with-loopholes—was a substantive one in both form and practice.

In this revision, the Corps defined "water-compelled rates" as those non-waterway transportation charges that are likely to prevail in the future if the waterway is improved; "non-water-compelled rates" are those likely to prevail in the future if the waterway is not improved. Given these definitions, the process of estimating future *traffic* required a comparison of expected barge rates after completion of the waterway and water-compelled rates on alternative modes. However, the basis of estimating *unit cost savings* moved back from the cost basis adopted (in principle) in 1960 to a position intermediate to it and the pre–1960 practice of using current rate differentials. The estimation of unit cost savings in this revision required the comparison of projected post-project barge rates and future, though *non*-water-compelled, rates on alternative modes. That is, the projected rates on transportation modes alternative to the waterway would reflect technological improvements in the alternative modes but not the competition of the waterway.

The following paragraphs, taken from the Corps engineering manual, explain this interim procedure.[25]

1. The traffic that would be expected to move over a considered improved waterway will be estimated on the basis of projected "water-compelled" rates with consideration of all data and factors that are likely to modify current rates to take account of the competitive situation anticipated with the waterway in being, and foreseeable technological developments applicable to the several transport media.

2. Estimates of unit transportation savings attributable to the waterway improvement will be determined on the basis of the projected "non-water-compelled" rates, with consideration of all pertinent data and factors, including the competitive situation anticipated in the absence of the waterway improvement, current rates, and foreseeable technological developments applicable to the several transport media.

3. The transportation benefits of a considered waterway improvement, for

[25] Perhaps the clearest description of these procedures and their rationale was presented on the floor of the Senate by Senator William Proxmire. See app. B for excerpts from his speech.

the movement of traffic that would move by other means in the absence of the waterway, will be derived by applying to the traffic movements estimated in (1), above, the unit savings estimated as in (2) above. These benefits will be used in project justification and in computing the benefit-cost ratio.

The effect of implementing this procedure was that estimates of traffic expected to move on the improved waterway were lower than estimates generated by earlier procedures. Because of the changes, fewer projects were able to demonstrate a benefit-cost ratio above unity. The response to these improved procedures by the Public Works Committees of Congress was one of strong objection. In particular, congressmen and senators from states with strong waterway interests found this interim procedure to be a severe obstacle to project approval.[26]

Through Section 7 of the Transportation Act of 1966, Congress, led by the waterway interests, eliminated the interim procedure. The essence of this legislation was to force the Corps of Engineers to revert to the pre–1960 practice of estimating both waterway traffic and unit savings on the current rate basis. The provisions of Section 7 of the act are as follows:

> The standards and criteria for economic evaluation of water resource projects shall be developed by the Water Resources Council established by Public Law 89–80. For the purpose of such standards and criteria, the primary direct navigation benefits of a water resource project are defined as the product of the savings to shippers using the waterway and the estimated traffic that would use the waterway; where the savings to shippers shall be construed to mean the difference between (a) the freight rates or charges prevailing at the time of the study for the movement by the alternative means and (b) those which would be charged on the proposed waterway; and where the estimate of traffic that would use the waterway will be based on such freight rates, taking into account projections of the economic growth of the area.

As a result of this legislation, navigation benefits are based on an estimate of future waterway traffic, which, on a priori grounds, is seriously overstated, and on an estimate of unit benefits for this traffic, which represents savings to shippers rather than the appropriate (and smaller) savings in national resources devoted to transporting commodities.[27]

[26] The objections of the "public works" interests in Congress to the interim procedure and the results of their objections are described in Robert Haveman and Paula Stephan, "The Budget Congress Won't Cut," *The Reporter*, February 22, 1968.

[27] It should be noted that savings to shippers as "construed" in the act is even an overstatement of the real unit savings that shippers are likely to experience. The real savings to shippers will equal water-compelled rail rates minus barge rates for future traffic moving by barge on the improved waterway and current rail rates minus water-compelled rail rates for future traffic moving by rail.

CURRENT WATERWAY EVALUATION PRACTICE—A CASE IN POINT

In order to contrast existing Corps evaluation practice (as required by Section 7 of the Transportation Act of 1966) with the correct a priori evaluation framework, the recent Corps analysis of the proposed Yazoo River Navigation Project is presented here as a case study.[28]

The Yazoo River flows for 169 miles in a southwesterly direction through the state of Mississippi. In its unimproved state it has a 9-foot navigation channel for about 46 percent of the time. The purpose of the proposed project is to provide a year-round 9-foot channel. Of the alternative plans studied, the "one-lock plan" was judged optimal. This plan would provide a 9-foot navigation channel for the 169 miles of the Yazoo River during the year.

The procedures employed by the Corps in estimating the navigation benefits attributable to this investment are as follows:

1. *Base-year potential waterway traffic* was estimated by means of a detailed study of the traffic flows in the area. This study was based largely on interviews with shippers in the Yazoo River basin area.

2. *Savings in transportation expense to shippers,* taken to be the difference between base-year freight charges experienced on alternative modes and current estimated rates applicable to movements on an improved waterway, were estimated on the basis of observed rail rates and projected barge rates.

3. *Projection of the traffic* that would use the waterway from 1975 to 2025 was based on index factors developed by estimating the growth of population, agricultural production, and manufacturing output in the pertinent region.

4. *Estimation of future savings to shippers* was obtained by multiplying the future traffic estimates (obtained in point 3), by commodity, with current (or base-year) rate differentials (obtained in point 4).

The empirical estimates obtained by applying these procedures are outlined in the following paragraphs.

The Estimation of Base-Year Potential Waterway Traffic

The District Office of the Corps of Engineers accepted as potential traffic for the waterway the *entire* volume of "water-adaptable"[29] traffic that moved by all modes in the relevant region[30] in 1966—the base year. In addi-

---

[28] The data and procedures discussed in this section are taken from U.S. Army, Corps of Engineers, *Review Report on Yazoo River Navigation Project* (December 1966).

[29] A commodity is treated as "water adaptable" if it is known to be moving on other waterways in the nation.

[30] The fourteen-county region surrounding the waterway was used for the study. This region is one of the least productive in the United States. In 1965, the per capita income of this region was only 46 percent of the national per capita income.

tion, because the project was not expected to be operational until 1975, all additional water-adaptable traffic expected to develop from 1966 to 1975 was included in the estimate of potential 1975 barge traffic.[31]

For the base year, the Corps estimated annual potential traffic to be 806,200 tons,[32] of which 465,000 tons moved in a downstream direction, and 341,000 tons moved upstream. About 70 percent of this traffic was composed of agricultural products, fertilizers, or oyster shells.

Using this estimate of 806,200 tons of potential 1966 waterway traffic, the Corps calculated the traffic that would be likely to move on an improved waterway. In performing this calculation, the Corps analyzed each of the component commodities in the total potential traffic estimate to determine if the expected barge rates on an improved Yazoo River would be sufficiently below current railroad (or alternative mode) rates, to cause a shift to the waterway. If the expected waterway rates were sufficiently below[33] current nonbarge rates for a particular commodity, it was assumed that 100 percent of that commodity would shift to the waterway. On this basis, the Corps estimated that of the 806,200 tons of water-adaptable traffic currently moving in the region, 768,400 tons (over 95 percent of the total) would travel on the waterway if it were constructed.

The Estimation of Savings to Shippers

Having an estimate of traffic that would move on the river if it were improved, the Corps estimated current nonbarge transportation rates[34] and expected barge transportation rates if the waterway had currently been in operation.[35] The difference between these two rates is defined as the estimate of savings to shippers per unit of traffic in the base year (1966). Aggregate savings to shippers were calculated as the product of this unit

[31] It is interesting to note that the Corps of Engineers, in conducting interviews on which to base this estimate, relied on "lists of potential shippers submitted by the Yazoo River Development Committee of the Rivers and Harbors Association of Mississippi."

[32] This estimate of potential traffic should be compared with the average annual traffic flow on the Yazoo River of 22,000 tons in 1935 to about 150,000 tons per year in recent years. According to the Corps report on the Yazoo River, the latter number was bloated by "movements by shipping interests in good faith to demonstrate their interest in a year-round navigation channel." As noted above, the Yazoo River is currently navigable at 9-foot depths for nearly 50 percent of the year.

[33] The determination of "sufficiently below" is apparently subjective and judgmental.

[34] The land transportation charges were obtained either from tariff records on file with the Interstate Commerce Commission or from rate scales applicable to similar movements under like conditions.

[35] This estimate was synthesized largely from barge-rate experience on other improved waterways, e.g., the Mississippi River or the Gulf Intracoastal Waterway. For example, while grain movements by barge on the Yazoo River are now charged $2.02 per ton, the Corps estimated that the barge rate for the same commodity and distance, *were the Yazoo River improved*, would be only 79 cents, or only 39 percent of the preimprovement rate.

savings and the number of tons of traffic that would move on the waterway if it were improved (discussed in the preceding paragraph). For the traffic moving upstream, the savings to shippers averaged 85 cents per ton, and for traffic moving downstream, per ton savings averaged $1.48. Thus, the total annual transportation expense that would have been saved by shippers if the waterway had been in operation in 1966 was estimated at $943,100.

To project this annual savings to 1975 (when the improved waterway would be in operation), the Corps added $49,000 of additional savings from the traffic that was expected to develop between 1966 and 1975. For 1975, the total annual benefit estimate was $992,000.

Projection of Future Traffic

The future traffic expected to move on the improved Yazoo River was projected by the Corps by the application of factors of increase. The base-year estimate of 768,400 tons of waterway traffic was scaled upward on the basis of projected changes in population and agricultural and industrial growth. The pertinent growth indexes developed by the Corps of Engineers for population, agricultural output, and manufacturing output in the relevant trade area are (1966 = 100):

	1975	2025
Population	108	202
Agricultural output	120	253
Manufacturing output (value added)	132	1,040

For both population and agricultural output, the rate of growth implied by these indexes is about that estimated for the entire United States by the Bureau of the Census and the Department of Agriculture. The rates of growth implied by the index for value added is about 6–7 percent, or about 150 percent of the rate of growth of projected value added for the United States.

To obtain the traffic projection for movement on the improved Yazoo River, the agricultural output indexes were applied to the agricultural components of the 1966 expected traffic estimate. The manufacturing output indexes were applied to the industrial components of expected 1966 traffic on the improved waterway. The population indexes were used to project the tonnage growth for commodities related to personal consumption.

The Corps projection of future traffic in 1975 and 2025 on the improved Yazoo River is as follows:

	1966	1975	2025
	(--------------------tons--------------------)		
Agricultural commodities	294,000	348,400	796,300
Industrial commodities	417,500	581,100	4,578,400
Commodities related to			
personal consumption	56,900	61,500	115,000
Total	768,400	991,000	5,489,700

Future Savings to Shippers

In projecting the stream of navigation benefits (aggregate savings to shippers), the Corps multiplied the projected tonnage figures, by commodity, by the unit savings to shippers. The life of the project was stipulated as fifty years, extending from 1975 to 2025. The expected annual benefits from an improved waterway are as follows:

	1966	1975	2025
	(--------------------dollars--------------------)		
Agricultural commodities	463,000	579,500	1,221,500
Industrial commodities	442,000	609,200	4,799,800
Commodities related to			
personal consumption	37,600	40,600	75,900
Total	942,600	1,229,300	6,097,200

Using an interest rate of $3\frac{1}{8}$ percent, the estimate of annual navigation benefits totaled $3,169,500. The benefit-cost ratio for the entire project was calculated to be 1.6.

As is clear from this example, the analytical framework applied by the Corps, and dictated by legislation, deviates substantially from the appropriate framework presented in the first section of this chapter. The Corps estimates of both expected traffic and unit benefits include substantial values beyond those economically justifiable. From this a priori analysis, there is a sound basis for claiming that the Corps of Engineers estimates of waterway benefits seriously overstate real national economic benefits in the form of reduced transportation costs.

A CASE STUDY IN EX POST EVALUATION: THE ILLINOIS WATERWAY

In this section, the results of an effort to evaluate the performance of a public investment designed to produce navigation benefits are reported. The investment evaluated is that undertaken by the Corps of Engineers on the Illinois Waterway. This evaluation of the realized benefits of a navigation improvement is designed to demonstrate the procedures required to develop an estimate of economic benefits and the difficulties in applying them.[36] It should also illuminate the serious weaknesses in the bloated estimates of ex post navigation benefits developed by waterway interests.[37] Because virtually no traffic would move on an unimproved Illinois River and because substantial survey data on the waterway have recently been developed by the Corps of Engineers and the Board of Engineers for Rivers and Harbors, the Illinois Waterway project forms an ideal basis for an ex post evaluation study.

The Illinois River flows from Chicago to about 40 miles above St. Louis, where it meets the Mississippi River—a distance of 327 miles. Over the past thirty-five years, federal funds have been used to transform the river into a navigable waterway. Currently, the river is navigable throughout its length and, with few exceptions, possesses a depth of 9 feet and a width of 300 feet. The geographic location of the waterway is shown in Figure 14.

The portion of the waterway analyzed in this study extends from the river mouth, at Grafton, Illinois, to Lockport, Illinois, a distance of 291 miles. The two remaining segments of the waterway, the Cal-Sag project and the Chicago Sanitary and Ship Canal, are excluded since the former is not yet complete and the latter was constructed by the state of Illinois for nonnavigation purposes.

The portion of the Illinois Waterway below Lockport has seven locks, each 110 feet wide and 600 feet long. Five of these locks were completed in 1933, and the remainder went into operation in 1939. For the purpose of this analysis, then, the project will be assumed to begin in 1939 and to last for fifty years.

In terms of 1962 prices, the estimated cost of the project over its life is $196 million. Of this amount, $185 million will be borne by the federal government and $11 million by state and local interests.[38] The vast majority of these costs have already been incurred.

[36] The only other systematic analysis of the realized benefits of a waterway improvement not performed or supported by a vested interest group is that presented by Frank H. Dalia. This analysis was a part of Dalia's Ph.D. dissertation submitted to the Department of Economics of Tulane University in 1964 ("An Economic Examination of Federal Water Resources Developments in the Ouachita-Black River Basin"). The Ouachita-Black navigation project was undertaken by the Corps of Engineers in 1922.

In this study, Dalia estimated that the realized benefits of the Ouachita-Black project equalled $2.6 million and the realized costs equalled $30,722,000. The resulting ex post benefit-cost ratio was calculated to be a minute 0.085. Dalia estimated that from 1922 to 1962 the sum of all undiscounted benefits (in 1962 dollars) was approximately one-third the sum of all undiscounted costs.

[37] See, for example, the data and conclusions in *Waterway Economics*, vol. 1, no. 3 (January 1967), published by The American Waterway Operators, Inc., Washington, D.C.

[38] This information and the raw data on which this analysis is based were obtained from the Evaluation Division of the Board of Engineers for Rivers and Harbors in Washington, D.C. The data were gathered by the board for a study of the Illinois Waterway in 1966.

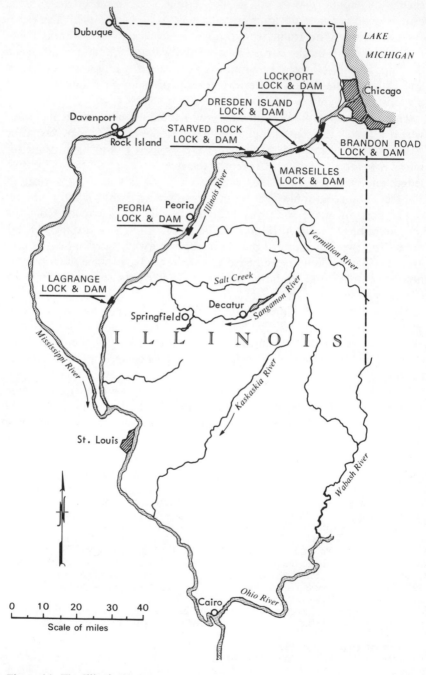

Figure 14. The Illinois Waterway.

In this study, an attempt is made to provide empirical answers to the following questions:

1. Given both the traffic that has actually moved on the Illinois Waterway and an estimate of future traffic, with projected future rates until 1988 (the end of its fifty-year life), how much have shippers using the waterway actually saved in shipping charges?

2. Given an estimate of the traffic that would have moved on the waterway if the rate differential between barge and the least-cost alternative mode were equal to the *cost* differential of these modes, what is the national resource cost savings attributable to the Illinois Waterway?

The answer to the first question yields a benefit estimate close to that of the 1964 Corps revision of benefit estimation procedures. The only difference is that actual nonbarge rates along the Illinois Waterway would reflect both technological improvements and the competition of the waterway. In the 1964 procedure, only the former of these effects would be reflected in the benefit estimate.[39] However, because the unit savings implicit in the question are based on *rate* differentials rather than on cost differentials, the benefit estimate will exceed that based on a conceptually correct definition of navigation benefits.

The answer to the second question yields an estimate of navigation benefits under circumstances that permit no units of traffic to move by barge if an alternative mode with a lower real cost exists, the point being that, under actual circumstances, an improved waterway attracts some traffic for which it is not the lowest (social) cost mode. This problem of a divergence in private and social costs is due both to the absence of user charges on the waterway and to the practices in rail pricing of the Interstate Commerce Commission. The data available do not permit the ex post isolation of this component of waterway traffic, so, in effect, it is assumed that this traffic yields zero (rather than negative) net benefits.

Consequently, while neither of these estimates corresponds directly to the appropriate concept of economic benefits defined in the first section of this chapter, the second calculation based on cost differentials is judged to be a close, although somewhat overstated, estimate of the real economic benefits produced (and expected to be produced) by the waterway. The traffic that is not counted yields no resource cost saving by moving on the waterway. In fact, the movement of this traffic on the waterway entails costs in excess of those required for movement on alternative nonwater modes. Were units of this traffic counted in the benefit estimate, they would

---

[39] It will be recalled that the 1964 Corps revision was substantially more sound than the evaluation procedure now used by the Corps, as required by the Transportation Act of 1966.

be valued at a negative cost saving, hence reducing the benefit estimate still further.

In answering each of these questions, an empirical estimate of two time series is required. The first of these series is the estimated annual traffic utilizing the waterway together with its commodity composition and origin-destination distribution. The second is the estimated per unit cost or rate differential applicable to each unit of traffic.

In developing the series necessary to answer the first question, the following assumptions were made and procedures adopted:

1. All the waterways connecting with the Illinois Waterway were assumed to be operational so that the navigation savings estimated were incremental to the Mississippi River System.

2. All traffic moving on the Illinois Waterway was analyzed from actual origin to actual destination. Alternative sources of supply of the various commodities were not considered.

3. The rate differential observed on each of twenty commodity categories in 1962 was assumed to prevail for each commodity for the period from 1939 to 1970.[40]

4. The rate differential calculated by projecting barge and alternative mode rates, by commodity, were used for the 1971–88 period. These projected rates were based on the assumption that a once-for-all technological change relating to trainload and high-volume barge movements of coal and grain takes effect in 1971.[41]

5. In estimating the traffic level, by detailed commodity, the following assumptions were made:

a. For the years 1939 to 1962, actual traffic volumes recorded on the Illinois Waterway, by commodity, were used.

b. For the years 1963 to 1970, individual commodity traffic projections, assuming no structural rate change, were used.[42]

c. For the years 1971 to 1988, individual commodity traffic volumes

[40] These observed 1962 rate differentials were obtained from a detailed study by the Board of Engineers for Rivers and Harbors. In this study, all 1962 commodity movements in excess of 10,000 tons, amounting to 76 percent of the traffic that moved in 1962, were analyzed. Some 400 individual commodities were analyzed from origin to destination. The average unit saving developed in this analysis was applied, by commodity, to the remaining 24 percent of the traffic. These differentials also include an allowance for handling and transfer if more than one mode is used in a shipment.

[41] These rate projections were proposed by analysts of the Board of Engineers for Rivers and Harbors. While the projections are limited to coal and grain movements, these commodities compose a sizable share of Illinois Waterway traffic.

[42] These traffic projections with no structural rate change were done by analysts at the Board of Engineers for Rivers and Harbors. They are based on assumptions of the rate of growth of demand for each of the detailed commodity categories in the region of the Illinois Waterway, adjusted for stipulated expected economic changes, such as the increasing use of nuclear power in the Chicago area.

expected to move on the waterway, assuming *projected* rates prevail (see point 4) were used.[43]

6. It is assumed that the origin-destination distribution of traffic in each commodity category does not change from the observed 1962 pattern.

On the basis of these procedures, an estimate of the volume of traffic in each of twenty commodity categories using the waterway is obtained for each of the fifty years of project life. These detailed traffic estimates are shown in table 6 for selected years. The aggregate volume of traffic is plotted as the upper curve in figure 15. On the same basis, a rate differential for each commodity category for each year of project life is secured. The estimated total saving to shippers in any given year equals the product of traffic moving and unit rate differential for each commodity summed over all commodity categories in that year. This series of total annual savings is plotted as the upper curve in figure 16.

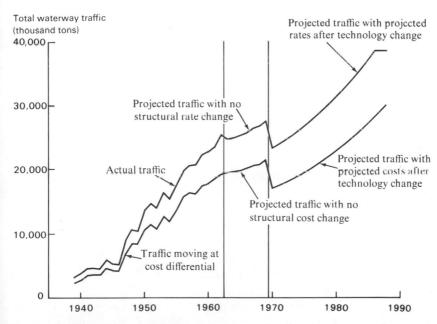

Figure 15. Illinois Waterway traffic moving at actual and expected rates and at actual and expected costs, 1940–1990.

[43] The traffic expected to use the waterway if projected rate differentials prevail was estimated by means of a detailed analysis of 1962 traffic in which those movements displaying actual rate differentials smaller than projected rate differentials were excluded. In this analysis, the ratios of traffic remaining to actual traffic, by commodity, were applied to the traffic projections expected to prevail with no structural rate change, by commodity.

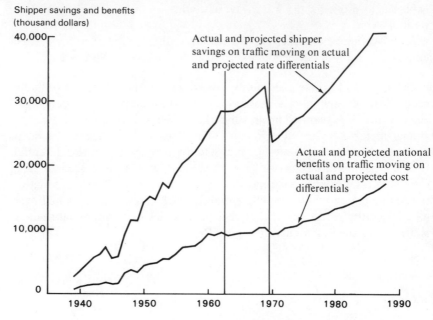

Figure 16. Shipper savings and national benefits on the Illinois Waterway on traffic moving on rate differentials and cost differentials, 1940–1990.

In developing the series necessary to answer the second question, the following points 3', 4', and 5' are substituted for points 3, 4, and 5 in the above list:

3'. The unit cost differentials estimated for each of twenty commodity categories in 1962 are assumed to prevail for each commodity for the period from 1939 to 1970.[44]

4'. Unit cost differentials calculated by projecting barge and alternative mode costs, by commodity, are used for the 1971–88 period. These projected costs are based on the assumption that the once-for-all technological changes discussed in point 4 above reduce costs by the same percentage as projected rates were reduced.

5'. In estimating the traffic level, by detailed commodity, the following assumptions were made:

a. For the years 1939 to 1962, actual traffic volume, by commodity,

[44] These estimates of carrier cost differentials are based on out-of-pocket costs of 1962 barge and alternative mode operations. These cost estimates were obtained from (1) a special study by the Board of Engineers for Rivers and Harbors of the Chicago and Illinois Midland Railway Company and the Illinois Central Railroad for railway costs, (2) an analysis by the Office of the Chief of Engineers, for barge costs, and (3) studies of motor carrier costs by the Interstate Commerce Commission, for truck costs.

TABLE 6. ILLINOIS WATERWAY TRAFFIC IN SELECTED YEARS UNDER ALTERNATIVE ASSUMED RATE DIFFERENTIALS *(thousand tons)*

Commodity group	Traffic on actual & projected rate basis					Traffic on actual & projected cost basis				
	1939	1952	1962	1972	1982	1939	1952	1962	1972	1982
Upbound										
Coal	1,720	4,201	7,808	5,764	8,033	1,410	3,445	6,403	2,542	3,842
Grain—Corn	371	1,039	330	392	467	235	659	209	249	295
—Wheat	57	48	189	242	310	57	48	189	242	310
—Soybeans	25	201	131	225	274	16	131	86	147	178
—Other	8	45	51	61	72	5	29	32	38	45
Petroleum and petroleum products	168	3,446	4,309	5,533	7,882	136	2,791	3,490	4,482	5,898
Sand and gravel	222	1,001	2,070	1,500	1,500	222	1,001	2,070	1,500	1,500
Iron ore	—	—	555	200	200	—	—	555	200	200
Chemicals	—	146	870	1,288	1,906	—	146	870	1,288	1,906
Phosphate rock	—	171	468	619	820	—	171	468	619	820
Other	240	889	1,651	2,443	3,617	171	634	1,177	1,742	2,580
Total upbound	2,811	11,187	18,432	18,267	24,481	2,252	9,055	15,549	13,049	17,574
Downbound										
Coal	—	89	5	—	—	—	36	—	—	—
Grain—Corn	80	752	3,258	1,799	2,700	32	552	1,209	1,646	2,510
—Wheat	18	433	388	497	636	18	173	388	497	636
—Soybeans	—	146	616	311	379	—	146	181	311	379
—Other	—	25	74	25	37	—	9	18	22	26
Petroleum and petroleum products	32	704	1,050	1,348	1,774	16	357	532	683	899
Sand and gravel	—	134	25	—	—	—	75	—	—	—
Chemicals	—	78	267	395	585	—	78	267	395	585
Other	174	492	1,248	1,886	2,791	136	448	994	1,471	2,177
Total downbound	304	2,853	6,927	6,261	8,902	202	1,874	3,589	5,025	7,212
Total, all traffic	3,115	14,040	25,359	24,528	36,315	2,454	10,929	19,138	18,074	24,786

excluding those movements that demonstrated no savings with rate differentials equal to the cost differentials estimated in point 3 above, was used.[45]

b. For the years 1963 to 1970, individual commodity traffic projections, assuming no structural rate change and adjusted to exclude those movements that demonstrated no savings with rate differentials equal to the cost differentials estimated in point 3 above, were used.

c. For the years 1971 to 1988, individual commodity traffic volumes expected to move on the waterway if projected rates prevail, adjusted to exclude movements that demonstrated no savings with rate differentials equal to projected cost differentials estimated in point 4 above, were used.

Use of these procedures generates an estimate of the volume of traffic that would have used the waterway for each of twenty commodity categories if rate differentials equalled cost differentials in each of the fifty years of the life of the waterway. These detailed traffic estimates are shown for a sample of years in table 6, and aggregate traffic volume is plotted as the lower curve in figure 15. Application of these procedures also yields an estimate of the rate differential equivalent to the cost differentials for each commodity category for each year of project life. The estimated total national cost saving in any given year equals the product of total traffic and unit cost differentials for each commodity, summed over all commodity categories in that year. This series is shown as the lower curve in figure 16.

In table 7, the benefit and cost results of this ex post analysis of the Illinois Waterway are summarized. The calculation presented there shows two separate estimates of the economic worth of the Illinois Waterway in 1939, using 1962 prices. Column 1 summarizes the results when observed rate differentials served as the basis for both traffic and unit savings estimates. Column 2 presents the results when observed cost differentials served as the basis for both traffic and unit savings estimates. In developing these estimates, the observed record of project performance during one-half of the fifty-year life of the project provided the basis for both benefit and cost estimation. In addition, projected changes expected to occur during the remaining life of the project, as observed from the perspective of the mid-1960s, were incorporated into the estimation model.

For each of the two traffic and unit savings assumptions, the present value of benefits was calculated, using both a 3 percent and a 5 percent

---

[45] The traffic excluded from the actual (projected) traffic estimates was based on a detailed analysis of the 1962 traffic movements. The question asked about each commodity movement was: "If the rate differential was equal to the 1962 cost differential would this unit of traffic have moved on the Illinois Waterway?" If the answer was negative, the transportation mode with the least real cost for that shipment was nonbarge and that shipment was excluded from the traffic estimate for the Illinois Waterway. Movement of this traffic on the Illinois Waterway entails real costs above the minimum and, hence, resource misallocation.

TABLE 7. PERTINENT SUMMARY DATA FOR THE ILLINOIS WATERWAY PROJECT

	Project evaluation using traffic on actual and projected rate basis and savings on actual and projected rate differential basis	Project evaluation using traffic on actual and projected cost basis and benefits on actual and projected cost differential basis
Present value in 1939 of benefits using 5 percent interest rate ($ thousand)	294.2	102.0
Present value in 1939 of benefits using 3 percent interest rate ($ thousand)	428.6	178.5
Present value in 1939 of costs using 5 percent interest rate ($ thousand)	233.2	233.2
Present value in 1939 of costs using 3 percent interest rate ($ thousand)	248.5	248.5
Benefit-cost ratio at 5 percent	1.26	0.44
Benefit-cost ratio at 3 percent	1.72	0.72
Range of savings ($/ton)	0.89–1.18	0.37–0.57
Median savings ($/ton)	1.06	0.48

rate of interest. When current rate differentials are used for estimating both traffic unit savings, the project demonstrates a benefit-cost ratio above unity in both the 3 percent and the 5 percent interest rate calculations. When the benefit estimates are based on the more appropriate cost differentials, the resulting benefit-cost ratios are substantially lower. In neither the calculation using the 3 percent rate nor that employing 5 percent does the benefit-cost ratio exceed unity. Using an interest rate of 5 percent, the present value of project benefits viewed from the year 1939 is less than one-half the present value of costs; on the 3 percent basis, the present value of benefits viewed from the year 1939 is approximately 75 percent of the present value of project costs.[46]

Table 7 also shows that, when existing *rate* differentials are used to estimate unit savings, the Illinois Waterway has reduced transportation expenses borne by shippers by more than $1 per ton in well over one-half of the years of project life. When the more appropriate cost differential basis is used to estimate per unit real resource savings, a median per ton value of less than 50 cents is found.

These ex post results are important both as estimates of the performance of the Illinois Waterway investment under various estimation assumptions

[46] A discount rate of between 3 and 5 percent was judged appropriate in evaluating benefits and costs from the perspective of the late 1930s—a low interest rate period. A calculation of the benefit-cost ratio using an interest rate of 10 percent—appropriate for the late 1960s—was also performed. Using the 10 percent discount rate, the ratio based on rate differentials was slightly above 0.5; the ratio based on cost differentials was below 0.2.

and procedures and as evidence of the extent of benefit overstatement that is generated by existing ex ante benefit estimation procedures. While the estimates in table 7 of the present value (in 1939) of savings to shippers exceed the more appropriate present value of real national resource savings, it should be emphasized that the savings to shippers estimation framework in this study is *substantially* more conservative than the definition of savings to shippers in the Transportation Act of 1966.[47] It should be recognized that additional data development and analysis could yield still stronger conclusions and provide more meaningful guidance to the development of improved ex ante procedures by public agencies.[48]

Suggestions for Further Ex Post Analysis

The nature of any ex post performance appraisal depends on the questions to which answers are desired. In the study described in the previous section of this chapter, an attempt was made to relate the actual costs of project construction and maintenance to the realized benefits of an individual project. No comparison between these results and the preproject evaluation was made. For other purposes, it is the basic benefit model of the evaluating agency that requires appraisal. For still other purposes, an appraisal of the traffic-forecasting procedures of the Corps of Engineers would be desirable. For example, if the analyst desired to provide feedback to the planning agency on the accuracy of its projection of traffic generated by the waterway improvement, he would have to compare ex ante traffic estimates with realized traffic flows or simulated traffic flows under varying rate differentials. On the other hand, if the analyst desired to evaluate the accuracy of the full estimation model utilized by the planning agency, the task would be substantially greater. Here, the task would expand to include an evaluation of the realized benefits of a project according to a theoretically correct model and a comparison of these estimated benefits with a reconstructed ex ante estimate based on the same model.

On the basis of problems encountered in undertaking the study reported

---

[47] It will be recalled that both traffic and unit savings in the savings to shippers framework employed here are based on observed and projected rate differentials as they exist throughout the life of the project. These differentials, therefore, are narrowed by both the post-project competition of the waterway and technological change in the nonwaterway modes. The Transportation Act concept of savings to shippers requires both traffic and unit savings estimates to be based on rate differentials observed prior to the project.

[48] These ex post estimates of project performance cannot be compared with ex ante estimates prepared by the agency prior to project construction. In the Corps report on this project, prepared in 1933, no benefit-cost ratio was calculated. In that report, "prospective" annual benefits were estimated to be $5.2 million, using the current rate basis. This "benefit" was achieved in the fourth year of project operation. Similarly, cost estimates were sketchy. For the Illinois Waterway, below Lockport, investment costs were estimated to be $15.5 million with $0.5 million annually for operation and channel maintenance.

on in the previous section, it appears that the next order of business for ex post analysis has to do with none of these purposes. Rather, it is the realized effect of project operation and pricing on which estimates are desired; in particular, shipper response to changes in rate differentials and rail rate response to waterway construction. It is judged that a cross-project study of the *realized* impacts of project existence on both these variables is required for improved ex ante evaluation. Cross-project analysis is proposed as a way of securing results insensitive to the unique circumstances of a single project. The following research efforts would be addressed to estimation of these variables:

1. Estimation of the behavioral response of railroads (and other modes competitive to the waterway) to waterway construction. It is often presumed that railroad rates tend to be reduced to a level close to marginal costs after the opened waterway begins to furnish competition. This phenomenon has not been investigated in a comprehensive manner. Ex post knowledge of this general behavior pattern is essential to accurate ex ante traffic estimation. Given the availability of detailed railroad rates, by commodity, this study appears to be a feasible one.

2. Estimation of the shippers' response to the rate differentials prevailing after the waterway improvement and to the rate response of the railroads to the improvement. This propensity to shift to water transport in response to rate differentials has not been the subject of systematic empirical investigation. This study would be a difficult one, because the natural growth of traffic on the waterway would have to be separated from the traffic shifting from alternative modes.

In each of these studies a particular variable in the appropriate model of project evaluation is isolated and subjected to cross-project analysis. It is judged that this ex post measurement approach holds out substantial prospects for securing pertinent information essential for accurate ex ante project evaluation.

CHAPTER IV

THE EX POST EVALUATION OF HYDROELECTRIC PROJECTS

Since 1938, the federal government has incorporated the production of hydroelectric energy into a number of its larger, multi-purpose installations. Among its currently operative facilities are some of the largest hydroelectric plants in the world. In 1968, about 8 percent of the nation's electric generating capacity was accounted for by federal hydroelectric installations. In a significant number of recent years, these multi-purpose projects received more appropriations than the total of appropriations allocated to single-purpose navigation and flood control projects.

In this chapter, two different approaches are used in the discussion of the crucial importance of ex post analysis and monitoring as a guide to ex ante project planning. In the first section of the chapter, an empirical analysis of the realized performance of twelve southeastern hydroelectric facilities of the Corps of Engineers is presented. The second section is a discussion of the need for ex ante benefit estimation procedures to account for technological change. It demonstrates the serious bias that is built into benefit estimates in which this variable is not properly accounted for.

Ex Post Analysis and Energy Output Estimation

Engineering techniques are employed for estimating the energy output and energy value of hydroelectric power installations. Through standard physical relationships between variables, such as stream hydrology, head, generating capacity, and the capacity factor, the analyst can estimate the average annual energy output (in kilowatt-hours) expected from a proposed installation. With even more sophisticated models and estimating techniques, higher moments in the distribution of annual energy output also can be predicted. Further, given information on the portion of the energy load that the installation is designed to serve, energy output profiles on a monthly and daily basis can be estimated for an installation. The following equation serves as an example of an engineering relationship utilized in estimating average energy output:[1]

If

P_k = average output per unit of time, in kilowatt hours,
Q = average stream discharge per unit of time, in cubic feet per second,
h = productive head, and
e = station efficiency factor, expressed as a fraction,

$$P_k = \frac{Qhe}{11.8}.$$

To obtain the value of the expected energy production, a price must be attached to each expected unit. This unit value, when aggregated over all units of energy output, yields the average annual value of energy produced by the installation.[2]

Clearly, to the extent that any one of the determinants of energy output (or any one of the several additional variables that determine them) is erroneously estimated, the final estimate of average annual energy output will be in error. For example, use of a hydrologic trace bearing an insufficient proportion of low-flow or drought recordings will yield an overestimate of average annual energy output.

In this section, some empirical results regarding the energy output performance of operating projects will be presented. These results will permit an evaluation of the predictive model employed by the Corps of Engineers. The results also should be helpful in stimulating a search by the agency for model inaccuracies, persistent aberrations in the application of the model, and other biases in the planning process.

The output results presented in this section pertain to the following twelve installations of the Corps of Engineers constructed since World War II in the Southeastern Power Administration (SEPA) power-marketing jurisdiction:

Allatoona Reservoir	Georgia
Buford Reservoir	Georgia
Clark Hill Reservoir	Georgia-South Carolina
Hartwell Reservoir	Georgia-South Carolina

[1] This equation is taken from William Creager and Joel Justin, *Hydro-Electric Handbook* (John Wiley and Sons, 1950).

[2] This statement of a need to attach a value to each unit of output ignores significant valuation problems. In practice, different values are attached to primary and secondary energy outputs and a special unit value is attached to the capacity itself. These values are taken to represent the value of the power to the users as reflected in their willingness to pay for it. They are obtained by evaluating the cost of energy and capacity from the most likely alternative source of power, usually a fossil fuel installation.

Walter F. George Reservoir	Alabama-Georgia
Jim Woodruff Lock and Dam	Florida-Georgia-Alabama
Barkley Reservoir	Kentucky
Center Hill Reservoir	Tennessee
Cheatham Lock and Dam	Tennessee
Dale Hollow Reservoir	Kentucky-Tennessee
Old Hickory Lock and Dam	Tennessee
Wolf Creek Reservoir	Kentucky

Of the twelve projects, the six located in Kentucky and Tennessee form what is known as the Cumberland Power System. Five additional projects form the Georgia-Alabama-South Carolina Power System.[3]

For each of these projects, the power output in kilowatt-hours was obtained from SEPA for each year of project operation. The time series of this physical output data is shown for each project and system as curve A in each of figures 17–30. To obtain the series for the power systems (figures 22 and 30), the observed output of each of the component units of the system is summed for each year.

Perhaps the most striking characteristic of these output patterns is their substantial variability from year to year. Of the projects that have been producing for six years or more, the Jim Woodruff project is the only exception to this pattern. A portion of the stability of this series is attributable to the fact that this project is located downstream from other installations that perform a streamflow regulation function.

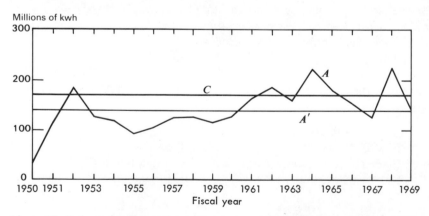

Figure 17. Estimated and actual annual energy output, 1950–1969—Allatoona Dam.

[3] The Southeastern Power Administration also has jurisdiction over the Kerr-Philpott System in Virginia and North Carolina. Analysis of the performance of this system is complicated by the purchase and resale of a substantial amount of firming energy which is indistinguishable from generated energy in the project report. This system is not analyzed in this study.

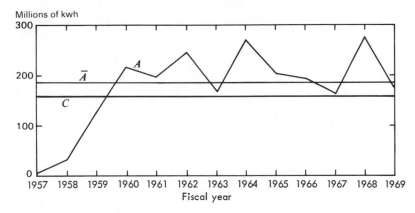

Figure 18. Estimated and actual annual energy output, 1957–1969—Buford Reservoir.

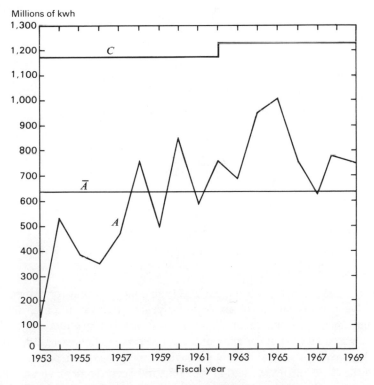

Figure 19. Estimated and actual annual energy output, 1953–1969—Clark Hill Reservoir.

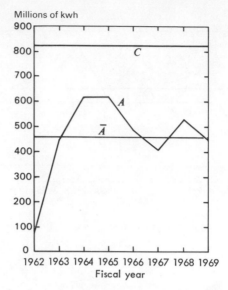

Figure 20. Estimated and actual annual energy output, 1962–1969—Hartwell Reservoir.

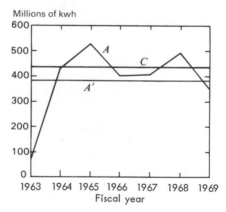

Figure 21. Estimated and actual annual energy output, 1963–1969—Walter F. George Lock and Dam.

Table 8 expresses this serial variability in energy output for projects that have been in operation for six or more years. It shows the high and low annual energy output (excluding the first year of production) and the average annual output for each of these projects. In figures 17–30, curve $\bar{A}$ displays average annual output for each of the projects or power systems.

Of the eleven projects listed in the table, five record a peak annual output figure that is in excess of 200 percent of the low annual output value. Both the Wolf Creek and the Dale Hollow projects record a high figure that is

TABLE 8. HIGH, LOW, AND AVERAGE ANNUAL OUTPUT, SELECTED HYDROELECTRIC PROJECTS
(millions of kilowatt-hours)

Project	High (1)	Low (2)	Average ($\bar{A}'$) (3)	(1) ÷ (2)
Allatoona Reservoir	225	91	146	2.5
Buford Reservoir	275	125	203	2.2
Clark Hill Reservoir	1,005	352	670	2.8
Hartwell Reservoir	612	410	507	1.5
Walter F. George Reservoir	526	353	435	1.5
Jim Woodruff Lock and Dam	272	204	236	1.3
Center Hill Reservoir	469	245	342	1.9
Cheatham Lock and Dam	203	139	153	1.5
Dale Hollow Reservoir	185	62	120	3.0
Old Hickory Lock and Dam	637	334	480	1.9
Wolf Creek Reservoir	1,203	319	769	3.8

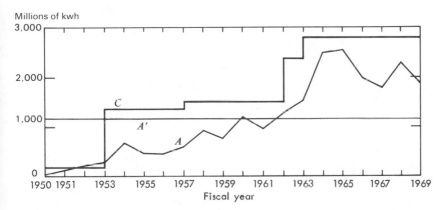

Figure 22. Estimated and actual annual energy output, 1950–1969—Georgia-Alabama-South Carolina Power System.

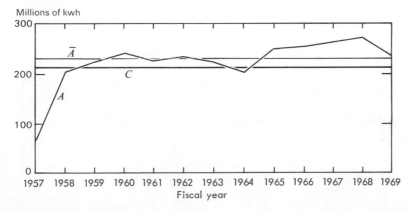

Figure 23. Estimated and actual annual energy output, 1957–1969—Jim Woodruff Lock and Dam.

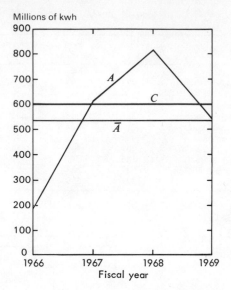

Figure 24. Estimated and actual annual energy output, 1966–1969—Barkley Lock and Dam.

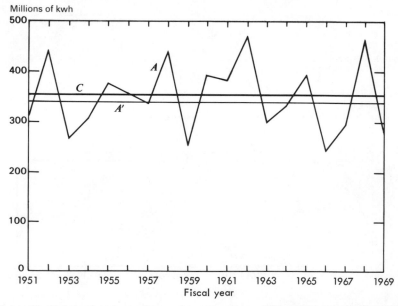

Figure 25. Estimated and actual annual energy output, 1951–1969—Center Hill Reservoir.

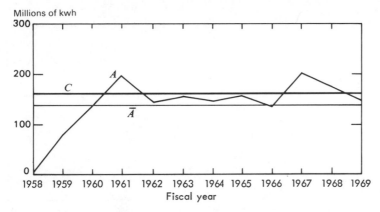

Figure 26. Estimated and actual annual energy output, 1958–1969—Cheatham Lock and Dam.

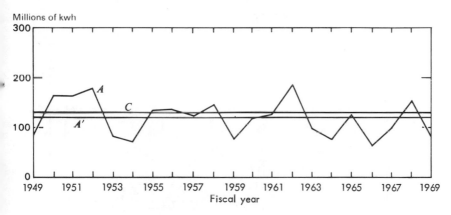

Figure 27. Estimated and actual annual energy output, 1949–1969—Dale Hollow Reservoir.

more than 300 percent above the lowest recorded annual output. With the exception of the Jim Woodruff project, all the installations show peak annual energy output in excess of 150 percent of the minimum recorded annual output.[4]

In addition to this substantial variation in annual energy output, one

[4] A primary cause of this annual energy output variation is the erratic nature of stream hydrology. In addition, for those hydroelectric plants with storage capacity, energy production can vary over time because of water allocations for downstream uses. Finally, some of the output variation may be attributable to the fact that most of these plants supply very little base load energy and operate primarily to meet peak load demands. The low value for some of the Cumberland System projects occurred in 1969 when a reservoir leak at Wolf Creek caused a drastic drawdown of the reservoir and a loss of power output.

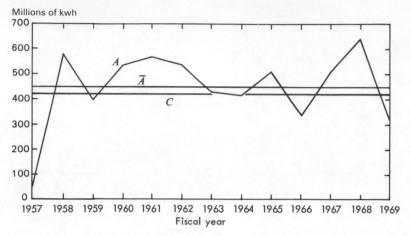

Figure 28. Estimated and actual annual energy output, 1957–1969—Old Hickory Lock and Dam.

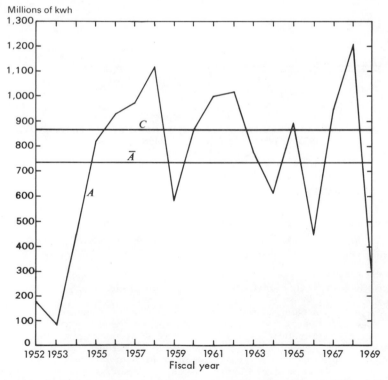

Figure 29. Estimated and actual annual energy output, 1952–1969—Wolf Creek Reservoir.

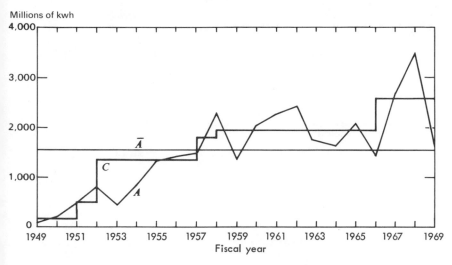

Figure 30. Estimated and actual annual energy output, 1949–1969—Cumberland System.

additional pattern should be noted. With the possible exception of the Clark Hill Reservoir, none of the projects displays any upward trend in annual output after the first year or two of production.[5]

With these data on the realized energy output of these installations, we can inquire into the correspondence of ex post results with ex ante predictions. In making this comparison, output results are related to the preconstruction estimates of energy output prepared by the Corps of Engineers and presented to Congress as a basis for decision. A number of assumptions were used to develop a statistic that could be accurately labeled "the ex ante output expectation." These alternatives are described in table 9 under the symbols B, B', and C, and estimates of them are presented in table 10.

Because of the significant time lag between the preparation of the survey report and project initiation and the significant design changes that often occur in this interim, statistic B cannot be regarded as a generally reliable indicator of the ex ante average annual output expectation of the decision maker. This is likewise true of the adjusted survey report estimate—B'. Although the adjusted value in some cases would appear more appropriate than B, the variation of the plant factor in response to alterations in installed generating capacity vitiates the general effectiveness of this measure as well. For our purposes, statistic C appears to be the most reliable indicator of the expectations of the decision maker concerning the future per-

[5] It is likely that the failure of markets to expand as rapidly as expected accounts, at least in part, for this absence of output growth. The rather distinct upward trend in annual output of the Clark Hill project remains unexplained.

TABLE 9. NOTATIONAL GLOSSARY OF STATISTICS AND TIME SERIES IN FIGURES 17–30 AND TABLE 10

Symbol	Meaning	Source
A	Actual annual energy output (in kilowatt-hours)	Data supplied by Southeastern Power Administration
$\bar{A}$	Actual average annual energy output (in kilowatt-hours)	Calculated from A
$\bar{A}'$	Actual average annual energy output excluding first year of project operation (in kilowatt-hours)	Calculated from A
B	Corps ex ante estimate of average annual energy output (in kilowatt-hours) as stated in the survey report on each project	Published survey report
B'	B with crude adjustment for alteration in installed generating capacity[a]	Calculated from data in the survey report on each project and in pertinent annual reports of the Corps of Engineers[b]
C	Corps estimate of average annual energy output at time of project initiation (in kilowatt-hours)	Data supplied by Corps of Engineers District Offices
C'	Corps estimate of average annual energy output for system at time of initiation of each project, excluding first year of operation for each project (in kilowatt-hours)	Calculated from C
D	Corps estimates of average annual prime energy output at time of project initiation (in kilowatt-hours)	Data supplied by Corps of Engineers District Offices
E	Corps estimate of the unit value of energy output (in mills per kilowatt-hour) as stated in the survey report on each project	Calculated from data in the survey report on each project
F	Power revenues (in mills per kilowatt-hour) attributed by SEPA to project	Data supplied by Southeastern Power Administration

[a] In making the crude adjustment, B, the average annual energy output estimate stated in the survey report was multiplied by the ratio of actual installed generating capacity to planned installed generating capacity. This adjustment assumed that the plant factor remains unchanged as installed generating capacity is changed.
[b] U.S. Army, Corps of Engineers, *Annual Report of the Chief of Engineers*, for the years 1946 through 1969.

formance of a proposed project. This statistic is supplied by the Corps of Engineers to Congress at the time each project is provided "new start" appropriations.

For each project and the three power systems, the value to which B, B', or C is to be compared is the average annual realized energy output—$\bar{A}$. However, because the first year of project operation either is not a full year or represents plant operation under the uncertainties of "start up" conditions, the average is also calculated in $\bar{A}'$ by excluding this first-year value. By comparing $\bar{A}$ or $\bar{A}'$ (realized, or ex post, values) to B, B', or C (expected, or ex ante, values) the relationship of actual to expected performance can be observed. In the following discussion, the relationship of $\bar{A}$ and C is taken to form the most generally appropriate comparison.

Table 10 and figures 17–30 suggest that a significant number of projects demonstrate a shortfall of actual to expected output. Of the twelve installations treated as individual projects, nine have yielded average energy output below that predicted by the Corps at the time of the appropriation decision. The extent of the shortfall, in terms of average annual amounts, ranges from 9 million kilowatt-hours (Dale Hollow Reservoir) to 535 million kilowatt-hours (Clark Hill Reservoir). The median average annual shortfall for the nine projects displaying a performance below that projected is 52 million kilowatt-hours. The ratio of actual to expected output $(\bar{A}/C)$ for these projects ranges from 54 percent to 97 percent with the median equal to 88 percent.

Excluding the first-year output results from the estimate of actual output (i.e., using $\bar{A}'$ in place of $\bar{A}$), the number of projects displaying a shortfall drops from nine to eight. On this basis, the ratio of actual to expected output $\bar{A}'/C$ for these eight projects ranges from 57 percent to 99 percent, with the median project producing 92.5 percent of its expected output in a typical year.

Using $\bar{A}$ and C as the appropriate estimates of actual and expected output results, respectively, only three of the twelve projects are seen to have generated more energy than was estimated at the time of project construction. These projects are Buford Dam, Jim Woodruff Lock and Dam, and Old Hickory Lock and Dam. The excess of actual over expected average annual output extends from 21 million kilowatt-hours to 58 million kilowatt-hours for these projects. The ratio of actual to expected output $(\bar{A}/C)$ ranges from 105 percent to 121 percent.

Replacing $\bar{A}$ with $\bar{A}'$ increases the number of installations displaying ex post performance in excess of ex ante estimates from three to four. The ratio of actual to expected output $(\bar{A}'/C)$ for these projects extends from 109 percent to 131 percent with a median of 112.5 percent.

Considering all twelve projects and accepting statistic $\bar{A}$ as the appropriate estimate of actual output experience and statistic C as the most accurate summary of expectations, the deviation of annual output expectations from realized performance $(\bar{A}-C)$ extends from $+33$ million kilowatt-hours to -535 million kilowatt-hours. The median deviation of actual from expected annual output is -25 million kilowatt-hours. The ratio of actual to expected outputs $\bar{A}/C$ extends from 121 percent to 54 percent with a median of 89 percent. Using $\bar{A}'$ as the best estimate of realized annual output, the ratio extends from 131 percent to 57 percent with a median of 97 percent.

Turning from individual project data to the power systems, similar results are seen. Realized outputs of one of the systems falls short of that projected by the Corps at the time of project construction. The actual output of the other system rather closely approximates the ex ante projection.

TABLE 10. REALIZED AND PROJECTED ENERGY PRODUCTION ESTIMATES FOR 12 CORPS OF ENGINEERS MULTI-PURPOSE PROJECTS IN THE SOUTHEASTERN POWER ADMINISTRATION MARKETING SYSTEM, AND RELATED DATA

	Allatoona	Buford	Clark Hill	Hartwell	Walter F. George	Georgia-Alabama-South Carolina System	Jim Woodruff
Date of authorization	1941 & 1944	1946	1944	1950 & 1958	1946 & 1953	—	1946
Date of initial construction	1944	1950	1945	1955	1955	—	1947
Date of first power output	1950	1958	1953	1962	1963	—	1957
Date of project completion	1950	1962	1954	1963	1964	—	1958
Installed capacity (*thousand kw*)							
Survey report	16	29	223	177	89^c	—	27
At initial appropriation	74	86	280	264^d	130	834	30
Actual	74	86	280	264	130	834	30
Estimated average annual project output (*million kwh*)							
B—Survey report	93	150	705^e	460	359	—	179
B—Survey report adjusted	429	445	888^f	685	524	—	199
C—At initial appropriation	171	155	1,173^g	818	436	—	213
D—Prime	91	120	475	365	280	—	144
—Secondary	80	35	698	453	156	—	69
Actual average annual project output (*million kwh*)							
$\overline{A}$—Actual	141	188	638	454	384	—	223
$\overline{A}$—Actual, excluding 1st year	146	203	670	507	435	—	236

Average annual system output (million kwh)							
C—At initial appropriation	—	—	—	—	—	1,654	—
C'—At initial appropriation, excluding 1st year	—	—	—	—	—	1,589	—
$\bar A$—Actual	—	—	—	—	—	1,112	—
$\bar A'$—Actual, excluding 1st year	—	—	—	—	—	1,169	—
$\bar A/B$	1.52	1.25	0.90[h]	0.99	1.07	1.07[i]	1.25
$\bar A/B'$	0.33	0.42	0.72[j]	0.66	0.73	0.66[i]	1.12
$\bar A/C$	0.82	1.21	0.54[k]	0.56	0.88	0.82[i]	1.05
$\bar A'/C$	0.85	1.31	0.57[l]	0.61	0.99	0.85[i]	1.11
$\bar A/C$ (for system)	—	—	—	—	—	0.67	—
$\bar A'/C'$ (for system)	—	—	—	—	—	0.73	—
A-C	-30	+33	-535	-364	-52	-542	+10
Average value of power (mills per kwh)							
E—Survey report	3.7	3.9	5.6	6.7	3.8	—	3.4
F—Revenue attributed by SEPA	8.4	10.1	5.6	7.5	5.0	—	6.4

(continued on next page)

TABLE 10. (Continued)

	Barkley	Center Hill	Cheatham	Dale Hollow	Old Hickory	Wolf Creek	Cumberland Power System
Date of authorization	1954	1938[a]	1938[a]	1938[a]	1938[a]	1938[a]	—
Date of initial construction	1955	1942[b]	1950	1942	1952	1941[b]	—
Date of first power output	1966	1951	1958	1949	1957	1952	—
Date of project completion	1968	1952	1960	1953	1958	1953	—
Installed capacity (*thousand kw*)							
Survey report	130[a]	90[a]	0[a]	36[a]	120[a]	270[a]	—
At initial appropriation	130	135	36	54	100	270	725
Actual	130	135	36	54	100	270	725
Estimated average annual project output (*million kwh*)							
B—Survey report	551[a]	328[a]	0[a]	120[a]	502[a]	867[a]	—
B—Survey report adjusted	551	492	0	180	418	867	—
C—At initial appropriation	600	351	160	127	420	867	—
D—Prime	NA	153	139	65	298	412	—
—Secondary	NA	198	121	62	122	455	—
Actual average annual project output (*million kwh*)							
$\bar{A}$—Actual	538	34	141	118	447	735	—
$\bar{A}$—Actual, excluding 1st year	653	542	153	120	480	769	—
Average annual system output (*million kwh*)							
C—At initial appropriation	—	—	—	—	—	—	1,561
C'—At initial appropriation, excluding 1st year	—	—	—	—	—	—	1,508
$\bar{A}$—Actual	—	—	—	—	—	—	1,524
$\bar{A}$—Actual, excluding 1st year	—	—	—	—	—	—	1,559

$\bar{A}/B$	0.96	1.04	—	0.98	0.89	0.84	0.96[i]
$\bar{A}/B'$	0.96	0.69	—	0.66	1.07	0.84	0.84[i]
$\bar{A}/C$	0.90	0.97	0.88	0.93	1.06	0.84	0.90[i]
$\bar{A}'/C$	1.09	0.98	0.96	0.94	1.14	0.89	0.96[i]
$\bar{A}/C$ (for system)	—	—	—	—	—	—	0.98
$\bar{A}'/C'$ (for system)	—	—	—	—	—	—	1.03
$A-C$	−62	−11	−19	−9	+27	−132	−37
Average value of power (mills per kwh)							
E—Survey report	3.8	4.7	—	5.0	4.1	4.5	—
F—Revenue attributed by SEPA	3.3	3.1	4.7	5.6	3.2	2.6	—

a Supplementary survey of system (including Center Hill) in 1947. Data supplied by the Corps of Engineers.
b Suspended during World War II (1943); resumed in 1946.
c The final construction of this project was based on a modification of the original plan. This figure refers to the planned installation for which Walter F. George was substituted.
d 333,000 kw ultimately.
e Decreases to 688 after Hartwell is constructed.
f Decreases to 866 after Hartwell is constructed.
g Increases to 1,225 after Hartwell is constructed.
h Increases to 0.9 after Hartwell is constructed.
i Median.
j Increases to 0.72 after Hartwell is constructed.
k Decreases to 0.51 after Hartwell is constructed.
l Decreases to 0.54 after Hartwell is constructed.

Using $\bar{A}$ as the best estimate of actual output and C as the best estimate of the ex ante output projection, the shortfall in average annual output is -37 million kilowatt-hours for the Cumberland System and -542 million kilowatt-hours for the Georgia-Alabama-South Carolina System. The ratio of $\bar{A}/C$ for these two systems is 98 percent and 67 percent, respectively. Using A' and C' as best estimates, the ratio of actual to expected output is 103 percent and 73 percent respectively. Clearly, the ex post output experience of the Cumberland system has more closely approximated ex ante estimates than has that of the Georgia-Alabama-South Carolina System, irrespective of the estimates of actual and projected average annual output that are used.

Of potentially greater significance than the investigation of the disparity of expected from realized physical output results is a comparison of the estimated *value* of power output with the realized value. At the bottom of table 10, a first cut at such a comparison is shown. There, for each of the projects and systems, the projected survey report unit power value in mills per kilowatt-hours (E) is shown as well as the per kilowatt-hour revenue attributed to the project by SEPA (F). While E surely qualifies as an ex ante estimate of the real value of power, F is essentially a bookkeeping or accounting estimate. It derives from the practice of SEPA of attributing revenue to each of the projects so as to insure that the cost of power production (as determined by the Corps of Engineers in a cost allocation study) appears to be covered. This assigned revenue, therefore, has no normative significance in establishing the social value of the output. Because the costs that must be covered by revenue fall short of the full costs of power production, the revenue neither accurately estimates the real cost of energy production nor provides guidance in estimating the real social value of project output.

Nevertheless, the patterns in E and F observed among projects are of some interest. In some cases, for example, it is possible to perform an ex post evaluation of the ex ante financial or repayment projections on a project or power system. Such an analysis would determine the extent to which revenues actually generated by the investment relate to the estimate of revenues expected at the time of project inception.[6] For the eleven individual projects for which data are available, the range in the projected unit value of power extended from 3.4 to 6.7 mills per kilowatt-hour. In part, this range is attributable to the fact that some projects have a higher proportion of high-value primary energy output than do others. The me-

---

[6] A few years ago, the Department of the Interior carried out such a financial analysis of the entire Missouri River Basin Project. It was found that "project revenues for the first twelve years of project operation have been only slightly over one-half the amount anticipated for the period." See U.S. Department of the Interior, Bureau of Reclamation, *Report on Financial Position, Missouri River Basin Project* (December 1963).

dian projected value is 4.1 mills per kilowatt-hour. The range in the unit value attributed by SEPA to the projects is significantly larger—from 2.6 to 10.1 mills per kilowatt-hour. The median value is 5.3 mills per kilowatt-hour.

In the analysis in this section, the realized electric power outputs of twelve Corps projects were compared to the ex ante estimates of power output presented by the agency to Congress at the time the projects received their first appropriation. While some projects showed an average output level in excess of the ex ante estimate, the bulk of the projects displayed output shortfalls. Moreover, the depth of the shortfalls was substantially greater than the output excesses.

In the next section, a rather different approach is taken to the role of ex post observations in improving ex ante planning. Instead of concentrating on variables relating to the observed performance of operating installations, this approach will highlight the significance of monitoring private sector experience so as to improve ex ante estimates of public project performance. Whereas this section of the chapter was concerned with estimates of the physical output of public hydro investments, the following section emphasizes the problem of valuing these outputs.

MONITORING AND IMPROVED EX ANTE BENEFIT ESTIMATION

The importance of monitoring relevant price and value changes in the private sector is decreed by the model employed by the Corps of Engineers in estimating the economic value of energy output. This ex ante estimation is known as the "alternative cost model." Because the observed market prices of electric power fail to approximate the social value of the electricity produced, a procedure for calculating "shadow" values is required. In the model adopted by the Corps, it is presumed that the demand for power is completely inelastic; that projected electric power "requirements" will be met from one source or another.[7] The benefits from the public hydro plant, then, are the costs saved by *not* having to construct the best alternative (likely, private) facility. In practice, the alternative chosen is

[7] Electric power rates are generally judged to be inadequate indicators of social value for three reasons. First, because the rate structure is typically a complicated phenomenon, there is no single price that can be taken to represent the value of the electric power generated. Second, the rate structure is regulated by the Federal Power Commission and, hence, any observed price is one administered with objectives additional to economic efficiency. Finally, each sale of electrical energy is made under monopoly conditions, insuring that the supply-side pressures on power rates differ from those associated with a competitive industry structure. For further discussion of the alternative cost model and a comparison of it with the other estimation procedures, see Julius Margolis, "Shadow Prices for Incorrect or Non-Existent Market Values," in *The Analysis and Evaluation of Public Expenditures: The PPB System*, A compendium of papers prepared for the Subcommittee on Economy in Government of the Joint Economic Committee, 91 Cong., 1 sess. (1969), pp. 533–46.

usually a fossil fuel steam plant constructed in an optimum proximate location.[8] Assuming that the rate at which power-generating equipment is added to existing capacity is "correct," appropriate application of the alternative cost model will yield accurate estimates of the economic benefits of a public project.[9]

Clearly, appropriate use of the alternative cost model requires close reference to observed output and cost variables in the private sector. A particularly crucial variable in the application of this model and one that requires ongoing monitoring is the rate of change in productivity of the power-generating facilities alternative to the proposed hydroelectric facility. This variable is a crucial one because of the differential lengths of life of hydroelectric and steam generation facilities. Because hydroelectric facilities are generally more long-lived than alternative steam plants of comparable capacity, the power flow generated by steam plants alternative to the hydro facility is produced at progressively lower costs over time as older capacity in the power system is replaced by newer capacity and as lower-cost energy production is substituted for higher-cost generation. This reduced cost of both alternative capacity and energy is due to the cost-eroding effect of technological change.[10]

In calculating the expected benefits of a proposed public hydro project, then, two variables in addition to the rate of technological improvement are important. They are the expected length of life of steam generating equipment (or whatever equipment is alternative to the proposed hydroelectric facility) and the expected patterns of phasing out and retiring the equipment used in alternative steam generation facilities. Each of these variables must be accurately forecast for each project evaluation if meaningful benefit estimates are to be obtained. Like the technological change variable, the forecasting of each of these must rely on the past behavior of the variable in the private sector and the extrapolation of this behavior into future periods.

Thus, it is the secular trend of past technological change in steam generating facilities (together with knowledge of current technological de-

---

[8] In the Corps procedure, it is presumed that the site of the alternative is sufficiently near that of the proposed hydro plant that cost differences attributable to power transmission are minimal. The savings in generation costs, therefore, comprise the bulk of project benefits.

[9] Use of the alternative cost model, however, requires that inputs to all alternatives be measured in uniform prices and that the parameters in the evaluation process (interest rate; federal, state, and local taxes; insurance; etc.) be identical where identical social values are involved. This practice has not been generally adopted in agency preparation of benefit-cost estimates. See Otto Eckstein, *Water Resources Investment* (Harvard University Press, 1958), pp. 242–44. Also see Federal Power Commission, *Hydroelectric Power Evaluation* (1968), p. 18.

[10] This phenomenon has become increasingly important since the assumed length of life of many proposed public hydroelectric facilities is now taken to be 100 years.

velopments) that must serve to project future cost reductions for those installations alternative to the hydroelectric facility; it is the past trend in phasing out procedures that must serve to project future equipment retirement patterns for the steam plant alternative; it is the trend in the length of life of steam generating equipment (in combination with an understanding of future expected changes) that must serve to project future lengths of equipment life. That is to say, each of these three variables must be persistently monitored and revised on the basis of the observed trends in order to serve as the basis for accurate ex ante public project evaluation.

The following discussion and the calculation based on it illustrate the impact on ex ante project evaluation of changed technology, altered patterns of retirement, and modified length of service of structures alternative to the proposed project.

Length of Life of Steam Generating Plants

From the advisory reports submitted to the Federal Power Commission and published in the 1964 *National Power Survey*, the following evidence on changes in the expected life of steam generating plants was obtained:

Most of the [steam] generating units . . . prior to World War II . . . . were ideally suited for peak load and standby service after they had been superseded by more efficient base load units. Consequently, some of this equipment has had a useful life of 35 to 40 years—in some cases over 40 years. . . .

In general, the projected life of steam-electric generating capacity installed subsequent to World War II is still in somewhat of a gray area. . . .

. . . it is believed that a retirement range of 28 to 38 years would cover many of the situations which occur under various circumstances. . . .

There is considerable reluctance, on the part of the Committee, to the establishment of a single number for retirement studies. However, if the Committee must identify such a number, it would select 35 years to apply to the type of equipment which will be subject to retirement by the year 1980.

Retirements subsequent to 1980 would involve the modern type of high pressure, high temperature equipment with critical metallurgy and complicated cycle arrangements. At present, it is the best judgment of the Committee that this type of equipment may be subject to a somewhat lower life expectancy—say 30 years.[11]

From this testimony, it appears that the average life expectancy of such equipment has been decreasing over time and that for equipment installed today in steam plants considered alternative to a hydroelectric facility, it would be reasonable to estimate an average usable life of about thirty years.

[11] Federal Power Commission, *National Power Survey* (October 1964), pt. 2, pp. 27–28.

Productivity Change in Electrical Generation by Steam Facilities

During the first sixty years of this century, the rate of technological change in the electrical generating industry has been substantial. For example, the price of residential electricity[12] has declined from an index of 250 in 1915 to an index of 100 in 1964.[13] From 1925 to 1950, the average residential power rate fell by 3 percent per year. According to the Federal Power Commission: "The industry's annual rate of productivity [output per unit of input, in constant dollars] improvement has averaged 5.5 percent since 1900, more than three times the rate of increased productivity for the economy as a whole."[14]

This pattern of technological change in the industry continued until at least the mid-1960s and, according to the *National Power Survey*, will continue into the foreseeable future. In that survey, the expected decrease in unit costs was attributed to reduced operation and maintenance costs, reduced fuel charges, and reduced fixed charges.

The following projected cost estimates for electrical generation per kilowatt-hour of electricity sold were prepared by the Federal Power Commission:[15]

	1962 (actual)	1980 (estimated)
	(-----------------cents-----------------)	
Operating and maintenance expenses	0.13	0.09
Fuel expenses	0.24	0.17
Fixed charges	0.48	0.37
Total generation costs	0.85	0.63

While these projections cover only the period to 1980, the Federal Power Commission in 1964 saw little reason to expect that the rate of technological progress in the industry would be retarded after that date. Although confident predictions were not available, the advisory reports to the commission indicated:

> By 1980 it is estimated that nuclear generation will be competitive [with fossil fuel generation] in nearly all parts of the country.[16]

[12] Based on 250 kwh per month.
[13] FPC, *National Power Survey*, pt. 1, p. 11.
[14] Ibid., p. 10.
[15] Ibid., p. 284, table 77. The estimates for both 1962 (actual) and 1980 (projected) are averages computed from data on actual plants, some of which are being phased out prior to retirement. Thus, for 1962, for example, a new and efficient plant put into operation would produce electrical power substantially more cheaply than 0.85 cents per kilowatt-hour.
[16] Ibid., p. 92. In these cost estimates, no account was taken of the serious environmental costs of both conventional and nuclear power generation.

The 1964 estimates of the level of nuclear generating costs in cents per kilowatt-hour (at the busbar) from 1967 to 1980 are summarized as follows:[17]

	Cents
1967	0.54–0.60
1970	0.43–0.50
1975	0.35–0.41
1980	0.32–0.38

In addition, there was some expectation that nuclear generating costs would be reduced from the 1980 estimate through the development of breeder reactors and other technological advances.[18]

From the perspective of the mid-1960s, then, it appeared likely that the past pattern of technological advance in the industry would be maintained in future years. However, during the late 1960s, a number of developments caused the optimistic outlook for technological change in electrical energy generation to be substantially modified. At that time, costs of both conventional and nuclear electrical energy production reversed their downward trend, with the cost increase of nuclear generation exceeding that of conventional fossil fuel generation. Among the forces that accounted for this change was the high rate of inflation during this period, which affected the costs of nuclear generating plants with particular force. Although this effect has been a major contributor to increases in the current costs of electrical generation, it says little about technological progress in this sector. It has, however, been accompanied by a number of real effects that indicate some slackening in the rate of productivity change in this area. Among these effects are (1) the failure of nuclear plants to perform at the level of efficiency at which they were projected; (2) sharp increases in the cost of fossil fuel due to reductions in the rates of productivity increase in the coal industry; (3) the failure of heat rates in electrical generation to fall as they had in past years; and (4) the increased value placed on the environmental degradation associated with electrical energy production— values that have gradually become internalized. Because of these changes,

[17] Estimates prepared by the Subcommittee on Nuclear Development of the Generating Stations Special Technical Subcommittee and submitted to the Federal Power Commission. See ibid., p. 89.

[18] This expectation continued at least until 1969. "AEC apparently has a very high degree of confidence that costs of the LMFBR (Liquid Metal Fast Breeder Reactor) can be substantially reduced to the point when it can generate power on a utility system for about 4 mills per kilowatt-hour in 1990 (constant dollars). The LMFBR apparently has potential for further cost reductions below 4 mills, with operating experience and continued development beyond that date." Milton Searl, "Prospects for PPB at AEC," in *The Analysis and Evaluation of Public Expenditures*, p. 1013.

it was concluded in a report to the Joint Atomic Energy Committee in early 1970 that the energy costs for new conventional and nuclear plants scheduled for completion in 1975 and 1976 would be between 6 and 7 mills per kilowatt-hour, with energy costs of nuclear plants exceeding those of conventional plants by about 0.5 mill per kilowatt-hour.[19]

Because of these recent developments, then, the prognosis for future levels of costs and technological change is uncertain. Efforts to project technological change and costs of the alternatives to hydroelectric power generation are now more difficult than before these recent developments. Nevertheless, estimates of technological progress and the costs of non-hydroelectric energy generation are essential if water resource agency estimates of hydropower benefits are to be relied on.

Plant Factor Reduction of Steam Facilities

The process by which the equipment used in steam plants is removed from the system base is the third crucial variable in evaluating proposed public projects under the alternative cost model. This is so because of the cumulative phasing-out procedures adopted by the electric power generation industry. A new steam plant facility added to the system base initially operates at a high plant factor, say, 90 percent. As time passes, however, additional facilities are constructed and added to the base. The generation costs of these newer facilities are lower than the energy costs of the earlier facility. Consequently, the earlier facility will be used at increasingly smaller plant factors, because energy can be produced at lower costs in newer, more technologically advanced facilities. Consequently, although equipment may be operative for, say, thirty years, it increasingly becomes phased out and replaced by newer, lower-cost equipment, beginning with the very early years of operation. Because of this steam plant retirement pattern, the relevant energy cost by which to evaluate the benefits of a hydro facility must reflect this increasing substitution of lower-cost energy for the energy of the original steam plant alternative to the hydro facility.

Federal Power Commission studies have shown that, historically, the plant factor of fossil fuel facilities has fallen to about 20 percent by the twentieth year of operation and to zero percent (retirement) by about the thirtieth year. Although confident projections of changes in this retirement pattern are not available, recent trends indicate that with larger units operating under higher temperatures and pressure, future plant factors will tend to remain higher in the early years of project life than has been true in the past. As stated in the *National Power Survey*: "The large units now

[19] Philip Sporn, *Developments in Nuclear Power Economics, January 1968–December 1969*, Report to the Joint Committee on Atomic Energy, 91 Cong., 1 sess. (January 1970). The conclusions presented in the report were supported by the 25 percent increase in power rates announced by the Tennessee Valley Authority in 1970.

going into operation [will] spend more of their service life in base load operation than has been true of previous units."[20]

TECHNOLOGICAL CHANGE AND THE ESTIMATION OF PUBLIC HYDROPOWER BENEFITS

As has been stated, the alternative cost model of benefit estimation defines public hydropower benefits as being equal to the present cost of providing equivalent power capacity and energy by an alternative means. In practice, this present cost is estimated by calculating the present value of the *current* annual cost of constructing and operating steam facilities that will yield power capacity and energy equivalent to that of the proposed project. By using current costs of steam generation, the cost-reducing impact of technical advance is not reflected in the benefit estimates of public projects. Clearly, the extent to which ex ante benefit estimates are erroneous is determined by the values of the three variables discussed above.

To demonstrate the bias present in current agency practice, the results of an alternative cost calculation *with* technological change will be compared with a calculation in which *current* capacity and energy costs are assumed to persist into the future.[21] In the technological change model, it is assumed that technological advance occurs at the rate of 3 percent per year, and that this rate of cost decrease applies to both capacity and energy costs. If the initial year of the project is assumed to be year zero, the reduced energy costs will begin to alter the calculation in year 1, as the plant factor of the initial facility is reduced from its original level because of new, more efficient power facilities added to the system in that year.[22] As the plant factor of the initial alternative facility decays over time, the lower energy costs related to improving technology will account for an increasingly large share of total annual energy costs. In the last year of operation of the original facility (the twenty-ninth year), only 3 percent of the annual energy costs will reflect the high costs of generation of the original facility. As specified in the model, the original facility is retired in the thirtieth

---

[20] Pt. 1, p. 75.

[21] This model is the same as that employed by John V. Krutilla in evaluating the power benefits from developing Hells Canyon. See John V. Krutilla, "Observations on the Economics of Irreplaceable Assets" (Resources for the Future, 1970, mimeographed). His role in pointing out the inadequacies in an early formulation of this model and in developing the final form of it is acknowledged. See also Gunter Schramm, "Relative Price Changes and the Benefits and Costs of Alternative Power Projects," *The Annals of Regional Science*, vol. 3, no. 2 (December 1969), pp. 27–46. Schramm applies a similar technological change model to a situation in which rising factor costs affect the value of future output from both the hydro project and alternatives to it.

[22] In this technological change model, it is assumed that the initial plant factor (in year zero) is 90 percent and that this plant factor is reduced by 3 percentage points per year. This yields a plant factor of 30 percent in year 20 and complete retirement of the facility in year 30.

year, at which time both the capacity and energy components of total annual costs will reflect the low-cost technologically advanced facility that will be substituted for it. At this future point in time, this new facility will be the alternative to the proposed hydro plant.

From the thirtieth to the fifty-ninth year, the capacity value will remain constant, as during the first cycle, but annual energy values will again fall as the plant factor of the facility installed in the thirtieth year is reduced and lower-cost energy is progressively substituted for the higher-cost energy of that facility.

A third cycle following the pattern of the first two will occur from the sixtieth year to the eighty-ninth year, and a fourth (partial) cycle from the ninetieth to the ninety-ninth year.

In using this model to calculate the total cost of a thermal facility alternative to a proposed hydro project, it is assumed that the capacity cost in year zero was \$13 per kilowatt per year, and the year zero energy cost was 2 mills per kilowatt-hour. An interest rate of 5 percent was used to calculate the present value of future costs.

This technological change model can be stated formally as follows:

Let

A = present value of costs of alternative to proposed hydro facility,

PV_i = present value of annual costs in year i of thermal alternative,

C = capacity cost per kw per year (taken to be \$13 per kw per year in year zero),

E = energy cost per kwh (taken to be 0.2 cents per kwh in year zero),

P = plant factor (taken to be 0.9 in year zero),

K = constant describing percentage reduction in plant factor per year (3 percent per year),

d = discount rate (5 percent),

r = annual rate of technological progress (3 percent),

h = maximum number of hours operated per year (8,760),

n = number of years of hydro project life minus 1.

For years from zero to 29:

$$PV_i = \left\{ C + \left[E(P - Ki)h + \frac{E}{(1+r)^i} Kih \right] \right\} \frac{1}{(1+d)^i}.$$

For years 30 to 59:

$$PV_i = \left\{ \frac{C}{(1+r)^{30}} + \left[\frac{E}{(1+r)^{30}}(P - K\{i-30\})h + \frac{E}{(1+r)^i}(K\{1-30\}h) \right] \right\} \frac{1}{(1+d)^i}.$$

For years 60 to 89:

$$PV_i = \left\{ \frac{C}{(1+r)^{60}} + \left[\frac{E}{(1+r)^{60}}(P - K\{i-60\})h + \frac{E}{(1+r)^i}(K\{i-60\}h) \right] \right\} \frac{1}{(1+d)^i}.$$

For years 90 to 99:

$$PV_i = \left\{ \frac{C}{(1+r)^{90}} + \left[\frac{E}{(1+r)^{90}}(P - K\{i-90\})h + \frac{E}{(1+r)^i}(K\{i-90\}h) \right] \right\} \frac{1}{(1+d)^i},$$

$$A = \sum_{i=0}^{n} PV_i.$$

The alternative cost model based on current costs, as presently applied by the Corps of Engineers, is given by the same equations, but with r placed equal to zero. In this case the model reduces to:

$$PV_i = (C + EPh) \frac{1}{(1+d)^i},$$

$$A = \sum_{i=0}^{n} PV_i.$$

The differences between the two models and the extent of overestimation present in agency benefit estimates are shown in table 11. The data presented there refer to hypothetical hydro projects with expected lives of from 10 to 100 years. The present value of economic benefits per kilowatt of capacity is shown for both the model used in present agency practice and the technological change model.

From the table, it is seen that the longer the length of assumed hydropower life, the greater the overstatement of project benefits yielded by the current cost model of the agency. While real benefits are approximately 84 percent of agency estimates when project life is assumed to be 50 years, they are only about 79 percent of agency estimates when project life is extended to 100 years. In some of the larger multi-purpose installations, the overstatement present in Corps estimates represents a substantial volume of the total benefits claimed for the undertakings.

TABLE 11. PRESENT VALUE OF BENEFITS ESTIMATED BY CURRENT COST AND TECHNOLOGICAL CHANGE MODELS FOR VARIOUS PROJECT LIVES, IN DOLLARS PER KILOWATT OF CAPACITY

Length of project life (years)	Current cost model (1)	Technological change model (2)	2 ÷ 1 (3)
10	232.3	230.4	0.99
20	376.4	360.7	0.96
30	464.4	428.8	0.92
40	518.3	450.7	0.87
50	551.7	463.1	0.84
60	571.8	469.6	0.82
70	584.3	471.7	0.81
80	591.9	472.9	0.80
90	596.7	473.5	0.79
100	599.5	473.7	0.79

Note: The values for C, E, P, K, d, r, and h are as stated in the text.

The table also demonstrates the impact of introducing plant capacity in year 30 with thirty years of accumulated technological advance incorporated into it. While the ratio in column 3 falls 8 percentage points in the first thirty years of operation, it falls by 5 additional percentage points in the next ten years. Although substantially diluted by the discounting procedure, this same ratchet effect is present in the third and fourth capacity cycles as well.

On the basis of this analysis, the crucial role of technological change and of private sector plant management decisions in ex ante evaluation of power benefits is seen. The improved practice of benefit estimation requires modification of the alternative cost model to allow for technological change and continuous monitoring and ex post analysis of private sector cost and power system operating trends.

CONCLUSIONS

This chapter has focused on feedback information that decision makers can obtain both from analysis of the performance of their own investments and from the ongoing observation of pertinent variables in other sectors. Both of these kinds of feedback can play an important role in improving the process of project planning and evaluation.

In the analysis of the first section, a majority of the projects studied demonstrated a shortfall in the observed output of power relative to the ex ante estimate of the Corps of Engineers. While inaccuracy and overoptimism of ex ante agency estimates are suggested, it should be emphasized that the analysis in that section is not a comprehensive one. Moreover, the analysis yields no clues concerning the variables responsible for estimation errors. Further research is required to discern the relative roles of the hydrology study, the load factor, and the demand for power in explaining the variation between predicted and actual outputs.

The second analysis focused on the ingredients of an accurate ex ante evaluation of project benefits when the estimation procedure is based on the alternative cost model. This analysis demonstrates that failure to consider variables, such as the length of life of the alternative venture, the procedures involved in equipment retirement for the alternative project, and the prospects for technological change in the alternative, must lead to faulty application of the alternative cost model. Overestimation of ex ante benefits is the result. The analysis suggests the need both for recognizing the importance of these variables in applying the alternative cost model and for monitoring on an ongoing basis the technology and management of the alternative facilities.

CHAPTER V

THE EX POST EVALUATION OF
PROJECT COST ESTIMATES

Recent application of benefit-cost analysis in the planning and evaluation of public expenditure projects has generated substantial criticism and suggestions for improved practice. The bulk of this criticism has focused on the following issues in benefit-cost practice: (1) the appropriateness of the benefit-cost ratio as a criterion, (2) the value of the rate of interest used to discount future streams of benefits and costs, (3) the treatment of risk and uncertainty components of project benefits, and (4) the empirical measurement of expected project benefits. However, another variable on whose accurate measurement benefit-cost analysis depends has been neglected. If economic analysis is to assist decision makers in choosing among alternative public expenditures, it is necessary that the fixed investment that is, project construction cost—and the annual expected operation, maintenance, and replacement costs be accurately estimated prior to the construction of the project. It is to the question of the accuracy of the current techniques for developing ex ante estimates of the construction costs of public expenditure projects that this chapter is directed.

While previous chapters of this study have dealt with the outputs, or benefits, of water resources projects, this chapter focuses on inputs. Because the inputs of projects are typically both more easily measured and more easily valued than project benefits, this chapter will have a substantially different "flavor" from previous ones. In the discussions of ex post analysis of project outputs, much space was devoted to the conceptual meaning of benefits. In this discussion, costs will be taken to mean project construction costs, a concept requiring little further definition. An effort will be made to compare ex ante cost estimates with actual construction costs, ignoring possible deviations of financial costs from real costs. Thus, external costs generated by projects and deviations of real from monetary costs due to

The collaboration of Mr. Tirrell Langworthy in the preparation of this chapter is acknowledged. When this chapter was circulated for comments, joint authorship was indicated.

93

unemployment or factor immobility will be omitted from the analysis.[1] In essence, then, it is the accuracy of the ex ante agency estimates of monetary costs with their ex post counterparts that will be appraised. Because of these assumptions, it was possible to analyze nearly 100 projects in this chapter; only single-project case studies were presented in previous chapters.

PREVIOUS EX POST COST STUDIES

In this first section, the results of several agency studies of cost estimation experience will be summarized.[2] In these studies, it was concluded that agency estimation practice has improved greatly in recent years. If one conclusion stands out in these studies, it is that the serious cost overrun problem that plagued the public works program in the late 1940s and early 1950s is no longer a serious problem.

The Corps of Engineers Study, 1951

In 1951, at the request of Congress, the Corps of Engineers undertook a study[3] of the ex post cost experience of projects, most of which were begun in the 1940s. This study compared the realized cost with cost estimates submitted at the time of project authorization for the 182 projects under construction during fiscal year 1951 and for which funds were requested for fiscal year 1952. The results of this study demonstrated that the cost of the 182 projects increased 124 percent from the time they were authorized by Congress until their completion.

Since a large number of the authorization cost estimates were compiled in the 1930s, it was expected that price increases would account for the lion's share of the cost overrun. In the Corps analysis, it was estimated that about 58 percent of the gross error was explained by price changes, 18 percent was due to modification in project scope from that specifically authorized by law, and about 25 percent was accounted for by other administrative modifications. In the study, which included information on the experience of the Bureau of Reclamation and the Tennessee Valley Authority, it was concluded that "it would appear . . . that no agency has been able

---

[1] See Robert Haveman and John V. Krutilla, *Unemployment, Idle Capacity, and the Evaluation of Public Expenditures* (Johns Hopkins Press for Resources for the Future, 1969), for a discussion of the deviation of real costs from money costs due to unemployment.

[2] For a more complete summary and analysis of various U.S. agency studies of their own cost estimation experience, see Maynard M. Hufschmidt and Jacques Gerin, "Systematic Errors in Cost Estimates for Public Investment Projects," in Julius Margolis, ed., *The Analysis of Public Output*, Universities-National Bureau of Economic Research Conference Series no. 23 (Columbia University Press, 1970).

[3] Robert E. Jones, *The Civil Functions Program of the Corps of Engineers, United States Army*, Committee Print No. 21, Report of the Subcommittee to Study Civil Works to the House Committee on Public Works, 82 Cong., 2 sess. (December 5, 1952).

to estimate with any degree of accuracy so that it can provide for price changes such as have occurred in the past 15 years."[4] The subcommittee judged that estimates based on preliminary studies are inadequate, and that such estimates of cost do not provide an adequate basis upon which to make a conclusive benefit-cost evaluation.

The Corps of Engineers Study, 1964

In 1964, the Corps did a follow-up survey[5] to determine if its cost-estimating results had improved since those revealed in the 1951 study. In this analysis, 184 projects completed between fiscal years 1961 and 1965, each of which entailed construction costs in excess of one million dollars, were chosen. For each project, the study compared the "escalated survey report cost" with the total realized federal cost. In estimating the escalated survey cost "the survey report cost for each project was adjusted by the application of appropriate price level indexes to reflect the cost at about the mid-point of the construction period in order to minimize the effects of inflation from the cost comparison."[6]

The escalated survey report cost of these 184 projects totaled $3,850 million. Total actual construction cost amounted to $3,144 million. The percentage deviation of realized cost from the escalated survey cost was −18.3. Of the 184 projects, 125 showed cost underruns, while 59 projects showed cost overruns.[7]

In its study, the Corps gave further consideration only to projects whose realized construction costs were at least 10 percent greater than escalated survey costs. The reason for this was that "the 10 percent increase over the escalated survey report cost is felt to be the minimum allowable contingency factor for normal project cost increases during the detailed design and construction phases."[8] Forty-three of the fifty-nine projects showing a cost overrun were in this category. These projects constituted 23 percent of the total 184 projects and 22 percent of the total realized cost. As a group, their realized cost exceeded their escalated survey cost by 33.9 percent.

In the study, price increases in lands and relocations, design changes, and higher than expected bid prices were cited as the primary reasons for the cost overruns of these forty-three projects. The Corps claimed that "poor estimating, as such, accounted for a very minor portion of increased

[4] Ibid., p. 19.
[5] Department of the Army, Office of the Chief of Engineers, Headquarters, "Engineering and Design, Project Cost Estimating—Civil Works," Engineer-Circular no. 110–2–1301 (February 3, 1965, mimeographed).
[6] Ibid., p. 2.
[7] See Hufschmidt and Gerin, "Systematic Errors in Cost Estimates," p. 273.
[8] Department of the Army, "Engineering and Design," p. 2.

project costs."[9] However, citing and subtracting the source of errors and then calling the residual an "estimating" error only semantically hides the fact that the original estimate was in substantial error.[10]

In the Corps study, several of the projects had been surveyed and planned before 1950. In order to reach a judgment on the accuracy of recent cost estimation procedures, Hufschmidt and Gerin performed a separate analysis of the sixty-eight projects in the group that were surveyed and planned after 1954. For the aggregate of these projects, the original estimated survey costs deviated by less than 1 percent from realized costs. When price adjustments were made, the 68 projects showed an underrun of 23 percent.[11]

The Bureau of Reclamation Study, 1951

In the congressional study of cost experience cited above, projects constructed by the Bureau of Reclamation were also analyzed.[12] Because the Missouri River Basin project of the Bureau of Reclamation was considered with a "tentative" estimate of federal cost, the bureau considered it in a category different from the rest of its projects. The increase in cost of the total program, excluding the Missouri River Basin, was 106 percent. The 1951 estimated cost of the Missouri River Basin project was 274 percent greater than the estimated cost of the project at the time of its approval by Congress in 1938. The major reasons given for the cost growth were price changes (30 percent) and design changes authorized by law (43 percent).

The Bureau of Reclamation Study, 1955

In 1955, the Bureau of Reclamation undertook its own study[13] of the efficiency of construction cost estimation procedures. The bureau's study covered 103 projects with an estimated realized cost in 1955 of $7.3 billion. This was 277 percent of the original survey estimates of $2.6 billion and 199 percent of the bureau's escalated estimates of $3.7 billion. Nearly 90 percent of the projects showed a cost overrun on both bases of comparison.

---

[9] Ibid., p. 1.

[10] The format of this study was interesting in that it seemed that the Corps was only interested in improving its cost-estimating performance to the point that overruns were eliminated. This points to the treatment of cost estimates as simply budget entries subject to scrutiny, rather than as key components in evaluating the true worth of individual water resource projects. From an efficiency point of view, an error is an error, even though an overrun may have more deleterious effects on the allocation of resources among projects than an underrun. Further, the Corps seemed satisfied with its cost-estimating performance, even though this performance is characterized by enormous variation in the accuracy of estimation among the individual projects.

[11] See Hufschmidt and Gerin, "Systematic Errors in Cost Estimates," p. 285.

[12] See Jones, The Civil Functions Program.

[13] Edward C. Altouney, "The Role of Uncertainties in the Economic Evaluation of Water Resource Projects," Report EEP-7, Institute in Engineering-Economic Systems (Stanford University, 1963, mimeographed).

The Bureau of Reclamation Study, 1960

In 1960, the Bureau of Reclamation undertook another cost estimation study designed to evaluate its cost estimation performance in the 1950s.[14] The results of this three-part study indicated that bureau cost estimation performance had improved markedly since the 1940s and early 1950s.

In the first segment of this study, 128 projects started between 1935 and 1960 were analyzed. This project group showed a 72 percent overrun from original estimated cost and a 49 percent overrun from escalated cost estimates. Over 75 percent of the projects demonstrated realized costs in excess of original cost estimates, while 63 percent showed cost overruns when realized cost was compared with the escalated cost estimate.

The second part of the study dealt with seventy-nine projects covering the same period of time but excluding the Missouri River Basin units and the Colorado River storage units. This project group showed overruns of 36 percent and 13 percent from original and escalated cost estimates, respectively. When realized costs were compared with original cost estimates, about 67 percent of the projects showed cost overruns. When escalated costs were used as the basis of comparison, 52 percent of the projects revealed overruns.

The third subset of projects consisted of the fifty-four projects that were surveyed and started since World War II. In the aggregate, the realized costs of these projects were 9.4 percent above original cost estimates. While about one-half of the projects had realized costs in excess of their original cost estimates, only 35 percent showed realized costs that exceeded escalated cost estimates.

AN ANALYSIS OF RECENT CORPS OF ENGINEERS COST ESTIMATION PERFORMANCE

In the remainder of this chapter, an analysis of the recent performance of ex ante cost-estimating procedures of the Corps of Engineers is presented. This analysis is based on data for 86 of the 100 water resource projects on which construction was initiated by the Corps in fiscal year 1956.[15]

Fiscal year 1956 was selected as the base year of the study for two reasons. First, after the 1951 cost study discussed above, the Corps of Engineers was severely criticized by Congress for its inadequate performance in

[14] This study has been summarized in Hufschmidt and Gerin, "Systematic Errors in Cost Estimates," p. 276.
[15] See U.S. Army, Corps of Engineers, *Annual Report of the Chief of Engineers*, vol. 1 (1954–55). The fourteen projects initiated in 1956 but not treated in this study were small projects (primarily navigation) for which the data either were not separable from other portions of the project or were not available.

estimating project construction costs.[16] As a result, the Corps made a concerted effort to improve the accuracy of the techniques used for developing ex ante estimates of project construction costs. The second reason for choosing fiscal 1956 as the base year for the study was the postponement of the Corps construction activities during the Korean War. The enormous number (100) of new projects receiving "new start" appropriations in that year represents the first major infusion of funds into the program since 1949.[17] Appendix C lists the eighty-six projects analyzed here.

The Method of the Study and the Data

The data used in this study were obtained from the *Annual Report of the Chief of Engineers* for fiscal years 1955–66. For each of the projects analyzed, estimates of ex ante and ex post costs were obtained. The 1955 Corps estimate of project cost served as the ex ante estimate and was compared with the total realized cost of the completed project.[18] This ex ante estimate was the latest Corps estimate of cost prior to project construction. From this information, the absolute and percentage deviation of realized from estimated cost was calculated for each project.

The eighty-six water resource projects were then divided into four categories, based on project function: navigation, flood control, multi-purpose and shore protection. A frequency distribution of the percentage deviation of realized from estimated cost was established for the projects within each of these categories.[19]

In an effort to refine this crude comparison, the estimate of ex post costs is adjusted to allow for price level changes during the period of construction. These deflated realized costs are then compared with their ex ante counterparts, and the deviation between them is calculated. Through this

---

[16] Jones, *The Civil Functions Program.*

[17] *Civil Functions, Department of the Army*, Hearings before the Subcommittee of the House Committee on Appropriations, 85 Cong., 1 sess. (1957), p. 57.

[18] Cost, in this study, is defined as the money cost of constructing and installing capital facilities. It excludes the operation, maintenance, and replacement cost of the project.

[19] Estimation difficulties of two sorts were encountered in attempting to secure individual project cost figures necessary to establish the frequency distributions. First, some of the projects on which construction was initiated in fiscal 1956 were additional features to already existing projects. In these cases the annual reports did not distinguish the estimated and realized costs of the addition from those of the project as a whole. For those projects on which the only work remaining to be done in fiscal 1955 was construction of the addition, the estimated cost was obtained by subtracting the total realized cost of the project until 1955 from the 1955 estimated cost for the entire project, including the addition. Total realized cost of the addition was obtained by subtracting total realized cost of the project until 1955 from the total realized cost of the completed project, including the addition. Second, some of the projects were not completed at the time this analysis was made. For these projects, the latest estimate of total construction cost is substituted for the total realized cost of the completed project.

procedure, the realized cost for each project is stated in fiscal 1955 dollars.[20] The price index used to accomplish this adjustment is based on the monthly *Engineering News-Record* "Construction Cost Index."[21]

Ex Ante and Realized Costs: Current Dollars

Table 12 presents estimates of total realized cost and total ex ante cost for the eighty-six water resource projects initiated in fiscal year 1956, grouped by project purpose. The final column of the table shows the percentage deviation of realized costs from ex ante costs. This evidence indicates that the overall cost estimation performance of the Corps is excellent on this set of projects. Considering all projects begun in 1956, an overrun of only 0.7 percent of ex ante estimated cost is demonstrated. While aggregate ex ante cost estimates accurately reflect aggregate realized costs, it should be noted that Corps cost estimation performance varies widely among project types. The significant percentage overruns on navigation

[20] For three of the eighty-six water resource projects included in this study, cost data by year were not available. In the calculation, all planning costs incurred prior to 1955 were treated as if they had occurred in 1955. It was felt that, given the crudeness of the price adjustment, any planning cost that occurred in fiscal 1956, or later, would be insignificant in the overall results. For projects that were not completed at the time this analysis was made, the total cost in 1955 dollars was calculated by subtracting the project cost in that year and deflating this value by the cost index for fiscal year 1967.

[21] The "Construction Cost Index" is given in annual and monthly averages with 1913 as a base year. From the monthly averages, a new index on a fiscal year basis, with fiscal 1955 as the base year, was derived.

Although the *Engineering News-Record* claims that its indexes have "over the years proven to be infallible as to direction and in normal times accurate as to degree," the "Construction Cost Index" may not accurately capture the pertinent cost increases for any particular water resource project.

This is true for several reasons. First, the index is based on costs in twenty cities of 25 hundredweight structural steel shapes, base mill price; 6 barrels portland cement, bulk; 1,088 M feet board measure 2 by 4, surfaced four sides, lumber; and 200 hours common labor, at local prices. This catalog forms a set of input items that only modestly intersects with the input catalog for most complex water resource installations. This is true especially for navigation projects. Second, because the items in the *ENR* index include those inputs whose costs have risen most rapidly, the index probably overstates the cost increases for most complex Corps projects. Consequently, if there is a long time lag between the initiation of construction of a project and its completion, use of the *ENR* index to deflate costs tends to overstate the importance of price increases in cost estimation errors.

Evidence of likely overstatement by the *ENR* index of cost increases on water resource projects is found by comparing the index with a recently developed composite cost index of the Bureau of Reclamation. While the *ENR* index rose approximately 4.5 percent per year from 1950 to 1966, the Bureau of Reclamation index rose at an average rate of about 2 percent per year. See Gunter Schramm, "Relative Price Changes and the Benefits and Costs of Alternative Power Projects," *The Annals of Regional Science*, vol. 3, no. 2 (December 1969), pp. 27–46, for a further discussion of the effect of price changes in project evaluation and for a proposed procedure for incorporating expected price changes in ex ante project evaluation.

TABLE 12. TOTAL REALIZED AND ESTIMATED FEDERAL COSTS FOR CORPS OF ENGINEERS PROJECTS INITIATED IN 1956, BY PROJECT PURPOSE, IN CURRENT DOLLARS

Project purpose	Number of projects	Total estimated federal cost[a] ($ mil.)	Total realized federal cost[a] ($ mil.)	Percentage deviation of realized from estimated federal cost[b]
Navigation	55	66.7	68.6	+2.8
Flood control	24	204.5	181.5	−11.2
Local protection	15	83.5	71.5	−14.4
Reservoirs	9	121.1	110.0	−9.1
Reservoirs, except Eagle Gorge	8	99.2	68.2	−31.2
Multi-purpose	6	433.3	460.4	+6.2
Shore protection	1	1.6	0.8	−47.0
Total	86	706.2	711.4	+0.7

Note: The U.S. Corps of Engineers initiated construction on 100 water resource projects in fiscal 1956. This table contains information on 86 of them.

[a] Cost is defined as the 1956 Corps estimate of the money cost of construction and capital installation. This value excludes operations, maintenance, and replacement cost of the project as well as all local cooperation and contributions.

[b] Plus figures indicate overruns; minus figures indicate underruns.

and multi-purpose projects were offset by the larger percentage underruns on flood control and shore protection projects.[22]

By dividing the flood control projects into the subcategories of local protection and reservoirs, additional characteristics of cost estimation are observed. These subcategories are also shown in table 12. Of the total dollar cost for flood control, reservoir projects accounted for over 60 percent. While the unadjusted percentage deviation of realized from estimated cost is similar for the two subcategories, adjustment for the cost experience of the largest reservoir project, the Eagle Gorge (Washington) project, indicates significant differences in cost estimation performance among subcategories within the flood control category.[23]

Tables 13–15 present the frequency distributions of the percentage deviation of realized from estimated cost for each of the primary project categories. For flood control projects (table 13), nearly two-thirds of the projects and total realized costs show percentage deviations from 0 to −40. The mean dollar spent on flood control projects was devoted to a project whose realized cost deviated by 34 percent from its ex ante estimate. For multi-purpose projects (table 14), the range was significantly smaller.

[22] In 1956, the Corps claimed to have applied the findings of studies on wind, tide, and waves to the construction of deep-water inland reservoirs. The Corps estimated that "hundreds of thousands of dollars over costs previously estimated would be saved" by the design changes they were able to initiate in the free board requirements of reservoir projects. It is reasonable to suspect that this improved technology may have had some influence on the observed underrun of project costs in the flood control category. See *Civil Functions, Department of the Army.*

[23] Of the nine reservoir projects, eight showed an underrun in the −38 percent to −27 percent range. Eagle Gorge showed an overrun of +68 percent.

TABLE 13. FREQUENCY DISTRIBUTION OF FLOOD CONTROL PROJECTS, BY PERCENTAGE DEVIATION OF REALIZED FROM ESTIMATED TOTAL COST, IN CURRENT DOLLARS

Percentage deviation of realized from estimated cost	Number of projects	Total realized cost ($ thousand)	Percentage of total realized cost
Less than −50	0	0	0.0
−50——40	2	7,884	4.3
−40——30	4	41,071	22.6
−30——20	3	15,652	8.6
−20——10	4	15,891	8.6
−10—0	5	36,665	20.2
0—+10	1	5,362	2.9
+10—+20	1	382	0.2
+20—+30	1	12,200	6.7
+30—+40	1	5,289	2.9
+40—+50	0	0	0.0
Greater than +50	2	41,088	22.6
Total	24	181,485[a]	100.0[a]

[a] Discrepancy due to rounding.

Two-thirds of the dollar cost was in the interval from − 10 to 0 percent. The average dollar appropriated to these six projects was spent on a project whose realized cost deviated from its estimated cost by 14 percent.

Table 15 displays the distribution of the fifty-five navigation projects initiated by the Corps of Engineers in 1956. Nearly three-fourths of the dollar expenditure in this category was devoted to projects with observed percentage deviations of between − 10 to +40 percent. The average dollar expended in this category was devoted to a project displaying a 25 percent deviation of estimated from actual costs.

Ex Ante and Realized Costs: Constant (1955) Dollars

In order to separate the effect of price level changes from other factors causing realized costs to deviate from ex ante estimates, all project values (both ex ante and ex post) were deflated to 1955 dollars.

TABLE 14. FREQUENCY DISTRIBUTION OF MULTI-PURPOSE PROJECTS, BY PERCENTAGE DEVIATION OF REALIZED FROM ESTIMATED TOTAL COST, IN CURRENT DOLLARS

Percentage deviation of realized from estimated cost	Number of projects	Total realized cost ($ thousand)	Percentage of total realized cost
Less than −10	0	0	0.0
−10—0	3	302,023	65.5
0—+10	0	0	0.0
+10—+20	0	0	0.0
+20—+30	1	58,000	12.5
+30—+40	1	45,701	9.9
+40—+50	1	54,700	11.8
Greater than +50	—	0	0.0
Total	6	460,423[a]	100.0[a]

[a] Discrepancy due to rounding.

TABLE 15. FREQUENCY DISTRIBUTION OF NAVIGATION PROJECTS, BY PERCENTAGE DEVIATION OF REALIZED FROM ESTIMATED TOTAL COST, IN CURRENT DOLLARS

Percentage deviation of realized from estimated cost	Number of projects	Total realized cost ($ thousand)	Percentage of total realized cost
Less than −70	0	0	0.0
−70——−60	1	59	0.0
−60——−50	3	1,089	1.5
−50——−40	1	21	0.0
−40——−30	7	5,589	8.1
−30——−20	6	2,945	4.2
−20——−10	7	6,786	9.8
−10—0	10	13,949	20.3
0—+10	8	784	1.1
+10—+20	4	7,995	11.6
+20—+30	4	15,081	21.9
+30—+40	1	12,242	17.8
+40—+50	1	293	0.4
+50—+60	0	0	0.0
+60—+70	0	0	0.0
+70—+80	1	28	0.0
Greater than +80	1	1,786	2.6
Total	55	68,647	100.0[a]

[a] Discrepancy due to rounding.

The degree of deflation adjustment made in any project's total realized cost depends on (1) the changes in the price level over the period of project construction, (2) the distribution of project costs over the period of construction, and (3) the length of the actual construction period.[24]

The extent and effect of price level adjustment on the deviation of realized from projected costs can be observed by comparing tables 12 and 16. While the flood control projects show an underrun of −11.2 percent in current dollars, they demonstrate an underrun of −17.7 percent in constant dollars—a change of 6.5 percentage points due to price level adjustments. On the other hand, multi-purpose projects changed from an overrun of +6.2 percent in current dollars to −15.1 percent in constant dollars—a change of 21.3 percentage points. Navigation projects, intermediate to flood control and multi-purpose projects, show a 15.4 percentage point change due to the adjustment for price level changes. While aggregate realized costs were 0.7 percent above ex ante estimates in current dollars, realized costs fell nearly 16 percent below estimated costs after allowance is made for price level changes.

Tables 17–19 present the frequency distributions of percentage cost deviations for the three major project categories. In moving from the

[24] Because the construction period for multi-purpose projects exceeds that for flood control and navigation projects and because large doses of project costs are concentrated rather late in the period of multi-purpose project construction, the largest adjustment for price level change occurs within this category.

TABLE 16. TOTAL REALIZED AND ESTIMATED FEDERAL COSTS FOR 83 CORPS OF ENGINEERS PROJECTS INITIATED IN 1956, BY PROJECT PURPOSE, IN CONSTANT (1955) DOLLARS

Project purpose	Number of projects	Total estimated federal cost ($ mil.)	Total realized cost ($ mil.)	Percentage deviation of realized from estimated federal cost
Navigation	53	53.5	46.7	−12.6
Flood control	23	171.8	141.3	−17.7
Multi-purpose	6	433.3	367.6	−15.1
Shore protection	1	1.6	0.8	−52.0
Total	83	660.1[a]	556.4	−15.7

[a] Discrepancy due to rounding.

current dollar to the constant dollar basis, the distribution of percentage deviation shifts significantly downward for each project category. This is reflected in the decrease in the median value (using dollars of realized cost as frequency) for each of the project categories: for navigation projects the median percentage deviation falls from +15 to −6, for flood control from −9 to −36, for multi-purpose projects from +10 to −13.5. Moreover, in moving from the current to the constant dollar basis, the dispersion of the distribution of projects by percentage deviation is substantially narrowed for each project category.

Although the adjustment for price changes indicates a more consistent cost-estimating performance in each project category than is implied by comparisons based on current costs, the range of percentage deviations of realized adjusted cost from estimated cost is still enormous. The favorable

TABLE 17. FREQUENCY DISTRIBUTION OF FLOOD CONTROL PROJECTS, BY PERCENTAGE DEVIATION OF REALIZED ADJUSTED COST FROM ESTIMATED TOTAL COST, IN CONSTANT (1955) DOLLARS

Percentage deviation of realized from estimated cost	Number of projects	Total realized cost ($ thousand)	Percentage of total realized cost
Less than −60	0	0	0.0
−60——−50	2	6,345	4.5
−50——−40	3	33,682	23.8
−40——−30	4	14,035	9.9
−30——−20	5	34,794	24.6
−20——−10	4	13,284	9.3
−10——0	1	136	0.0
0——+10	1	352	0.2
+10——+20	1	4,424	3.1
+20——+30	0	0	0.0
+30——+40	1	30,758	21.7
+40——+50	0	0	0.0
+50——+60	1	3,433	2.4
Greater than +60	0	0	0.0
Total	23	141,243	100.0[a]

[a] Discrepancy due to rounding.

TABLE 18. FREQUENCY DISTRIBUTION OF MULTI-PURPOSE PROJECTS, BY PERCENTAGE DEVIATION OF REALIZED ADJUSTED COST FROM ESTIMATED TOTAL COST, IN CONSTANT (1955) DOLLARS

Percentage deviation of realized from estimated cost	Number of projects	Total realized cost ($ thousand)	Percentage of total realized cost
Less than −30	0	0	0.0
−30—−20	2	174,986	47.6
−20—−10	1	70,125	19.0
−10—0	1	43,217	11.7
0—+10	0	0	0.0
+10—+20	2	79,285	21.5
+20—+30	0	0	0.0
Greater than +30	0	0	0.0
Total	6	367,613	100.0[a]

[a] Discrepancy due to rounding.

TABLE 19. FREQUENCY DISTRIBUTION OF NAVIGATION PROJECTS, BY PERCENTAGE DEVIATION OF REALIZED ADJUSTED COST FROM ESTIMATED TOTAL COST, IN CONSTANT (1955) DOLLARS

Percentage deviation of realized from estimated cost	Number of projects	Total realized cost ($ thousand)	Percentage of total realized cost
Less than −70	0	0	0.0
−70—−60	2	90	0.1
−60—−50	1	905	1.9
−50—−40	4	1,378	2.9
−40—−30	7	5,233	11.2
−30—−20	5	5,135	10.9
−20—−10	10	3,319	7.1
−10—0	14	14,649	31.3
0—+10	6	14,098	30.1
+10—+20	1	75	0.1
+20—+30	1	247	0.5
+30—+40	0	0	0.0
+40—+50	0	0	0.0
+50—+60	1	26	0.0
+60—+70	0	0	0.0
Greater than +70	1	1,545	3.3
Total	53	46,700	100.0[a]

[a] Discrepancy due to rounding.

cost estimation performance of each project category and for the total of all projects is a result of offsetting errors, rather than of a consistently accurate cost estimation procedure.

Some Summary Statistics

Table 20 presents a series of summary statistics on Corps cost estimation performance in both current and constant prices. These data summarize a number of the patterns observed in the frequency distributions of tables 13–15 and 17–19.

TABLE 20. SUMMARY STATISTICS ON COST ESTIMATION ERRORS, BY PROJECT CATEGORY, IN CURRENT AND CONSTANT (1955) DOLLARS

Item	Current dollars			Constant (1955) dollars		
	Navigation	Flood control	Multi-purpose	Navigation	Flood control	Multi-purpose
Number of projects[a]	55	24	6	53	23	6
Mean percentage deviation	25.0	34.0	14.0	19.0	36.0	14.0
Median percentage deviation (by project)	−6.0	−13.0	−8.5	11.0	−12.0	−13.5
Median percentage deviation (by dollars expended)	15.0	−9.0	10.0	−6.0	−36.0	−13.5
Number of overruns (projects)	20	6	3	10	4	2
Greatest overrun (percentage deviation)	+129	+84	+46	+98	+57	+13
Number of underruns (projects)	35	18	3	43	19	4
Greatest underrun (percentage deviation)	−64	−50	−5	−66	−58	−25
Performance coefficient[b]	1.06	0.71	1.42	0.92	0.85	1.57

[a] The attribute used in computing this statistic is the absolute value of the percentage deviation of estimated from realized cost stated in dollars. The number of dollars of realized cost was used as frequency in computing the mean deviation.
[b] The performance coefficient is defined as follows:

$$\text{Performance coefficient} = \frac{\text{Number of overruns in group}}{\text{All overruns}} \div \frac{\text{Number of projects in group}}{\text{All projects}}$$

If coefficient = 1, group has same share of overruns and of projects.
> 1, group has a greater proportion of overruns than of projects.
< 1, group has a smaller proportion of overruns than of projects.

See Maynard M. Hufschmidt and Jacques Gerin, "Systematic Errors in Cost Estimates for Public Investment Projects," in Julius Margolis, ed., *The Analysis of Public Output*, Universities-National Bureau of Economic Research Conference Series no. 23 (Columbia University Press, 1970), p. 306.

The substantial disparity in cost estimation performance among the project types is clearly seen in the statistics on average percentage deviation. For example, in constant cost terms, the median dollar spent for navigation facilities was spent on a project whose ex ante costs deviated by 6 percent from realized costs; the median dollar spent for flood control facilities was allocated to a project showing a 36 percent deviation. The range of mean percentage deviation among project types is approximately 20 percentage points on both the constant and current cost comparison basis.

Table 20 also indicates that within the project categories themselves the variation of cost estimation performance is substantial. The range of percentage deviation (in current dollars) among flood control projects is from −50 percent to +84 percent; for multi-purpose projects from −5 percent to +46 percent; for navigation projects from −64 percent to +129 percent.[25] The mean deviation of the flood control distribution in both constant and current dollars is more than double the mean deviation of the distribution of multi-purpose projects.

The last row of the table indicates that the cost estimation performance on multi-purpose projects is the poorest of the three categories in terms of persistent ex ante cost underestimation. The percentage of projects in this category showing cost overruns is greater than in either of the other categories, in both constant and current dollars. This result is based on a comparison of the performance coefficient among categories.[26] In both current and constant dollars, multi-purpose projects show a performance coefficient that is about 50 percent greater than that for either navigation or flood control projects. From these data, it is evident that the excellent record of cost estimation for the group of projects as a whole is the result of substantial offsetting errors in cost estimation, rather than of a cost estimation technique that achieves equally consistent results within or among project categories.

Finally, the summary data of table 21 and figure 31 permit a number of additional comparisons. While, in current dollar terms, the entire group of projects showed an aggregate overrun of 0.7 percent (table 12), the eighty-three water resource projects for which price adjustments were made showed an aggregate cost *underrun* of 15.7 percent (table 16). While 33.7 percent of the projects showed cost overruns on the current cost basis, only 18.9 percent of the projects showed overruns when adjustment was made for price level changes. Similarly, in current dollars, 36 percent of federal

[25] When the comparison is stated in constant dollars, these ranges are −58 percent to +57 percent, −25 percent to +13 percent, −66 percent to +98 percent, respectively.
[26] This statistic summarizes the extent of cost underestimation in each project category relative to the extent of cost underestimation for all of the projects analyzed.

TABLE 21. FREQUENCY DISTRIBUTION OF PERCENTAGE DEVIATION OF REALIZED COST FROM ESTIMATED COST, ALL PROJECTS, IN CURRENT AND CONSTANT (1955) DOLLARS

Percentage deviation of realized from estimated cost	Current dollars			Constant (1955) dollars		
	Number of projects	Total realized cost ($ mil.)	Percentage of total realized cost	Number of projects	Total realized cost ($ mil.)	Percentage of total realized cost
Less than −70	0	0.0	0.0	0	0.0	0.0
−70—−60	1	0.1	0.0	2	0.1	0.0
−60—−50	3	1.1	0.1	4	8.1	1.4
−50—−40	4	8.7	1.2	7	35.1	6.3
−40—−30	11	46.7	6.5	11	19.3	3.4
−30—−20	9	18.6	2.6	12	214.9	38.6
−20—−10	11	22.7	3.1	15	86.7	15.5
−10—0	18	352.6	49.5	16	58.0	10.4
0—+10	9	6.1	0.8	7	14.4	2.5
+10—+20	5	8.4	1.1	4	83.8	15.0
+20—+30	6	85.3	11.9	1	0.2	0.0
+30—+40	3	63.2	8.8	1	30.8	5.5
+40—+50	2	55.0	7.7			
+50—+60	0	0.0	0.0			
+60—+70	1	37.0	5.2	3	5.8	0.8
Greater than +70	3	5.9	0.8			
Total	86	711.4	100.0[a]	83	556.4[a]	100.0[a]

[a] Discrepancy due to rounding.

cost went to projects with cost overruns, while in constant dollars only 24 percent of federal cost supported such projects.

Figure 31 and table 21 also show that the current cost frequency distribution is substantially less concentrated than the constant cost distribution. While the extreme negative values in the current cost frequency distribution were altered little by the deflation for price changes, the extreme positive values fell substantially. The constant cost distribution indicates that only 1 percent of the dollar expenditure was on projects showing an overrun of greater than 40 percent, while the current cost distribution shows that 14 percent of the dollar expenditure went to projects with realized costs of more than 40 percent of ex ante estimates.[27]

SUMMARY AND CONCLUSIONS

Agency estimates of the construction cost of individual water resource projects serve two purposes. First, project cost estimates are essential to ex ante analysis of the economic worth of proposed investments. Second, summed together, project cost estimates substantially influence the annual budget requests of the agency.

[27] This result reflects the fact that projects showing extreme underruns tended to have much shorter construction periods than those showing extreme overruns.

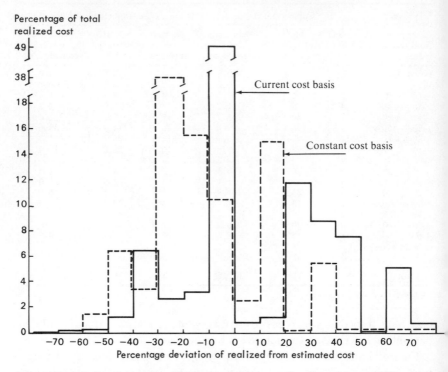

Figure 31. Relative frequency distribution of cost estimation errors on Corps of Engineers projects initiated in fiscal year 1956, current and constant dollar basis.

This study has illuminated two primary characteristics of the recent cost estimation experience of the Corps of Engineers. First, the cost estimation procedure of the Corps is characterized by enormous inconsistency in achieving accurate cost estimates for individual water resource projects. Second, the agency has achieved significant improvement in its ability to provide accurate ex ante estimates of the construction cost of the entire program of water resource projects.

In short, although the cost estimation results of the Corps have improved greatly since the 1951 study, the analysis presented here indicates that a substantial variance of error still persists. To the extent that the wide range of percentage deviation of realized cost from estimated cost is not due to a change in project scope or purpose, major opportunities exist to reduce this range by improved methods of planning and cost estimation.

More important, until more improved techniques are developed for the estimation of construction cost, an accurate appraisal of the ex ante economic value of projects is impossible. The enormous variation of ex ante cost estimates relative to realized expenditures erodes any serious reliance on benefit-cost calculations as a basis for project choice.[28]

[28] One possible way of reflecting this uncertainty in cost estimates is through the use of uncertainty allowances in expected costs. If uncertainty is a cost to the community, differential increases in ex ante cost estimates should be made. The variation of predicted from realized estimates for the project category could serve as the basis for the differential allowance. For a more complete discussion of differential allowance to adjust for uncertainty differentials among project types, see Robert Haveman, *Water Resource Investment and the Public Interest* (Vanderbilt University Press, 1965), pp. 156–76. See also Jack Hirshleifer and David Shapiro, "The Treatment of Risk and Uncertainty," in *The Analysis and Evaluation of Public Expenditures: The PPB System*, A compendium of papers prepared for the Subcommittee on Economy in Government of the Joint Economic Committee, 91 Cong., 1 sess. (1969), pp. 505–30, for a discussion of alternative approaches to accounting for uncertainty in public expenditure analysis.

EPILOGUE

This study was undertaken to establish a conceptual framework for the ex post appraisal of the economic performance of public sector investments and to make a first cut empirical evaluation of a few projects. The framework adopted in this study was based on a national accounting stance and emphasized the primary, or efficiency, benefits and costs of public undertakings.

The purpose for adopting this economic efficiency framework in appraising water resources investments was twofold. First, the basic non-political reason why government undertakes these public works activities is an economic efficiency reason. Were it not for the public good and the decreasing cost aspects of these investments, they would be part and parcel of the private sector and subject to the maximum net benefits criterion that guides private decisions. Because these activities do not typically serve social functions other than the correction of market failure, and because of the desire to avoid transferring resources from more productive activities in the private sector to less productive activities in the public sector, this criterion is also an appropriate one for these public works undertakings.

Second, the parameters of the production function implicit in the economic efficiency model are relatively well known. While there are still some unsettled conceptual and empirical issues, there is wide agreement on the definitions and measurement of inputs and outputs—of benefits and costs —within the efficiency model. The same cannot be claimed for other non-efficiency evaluation models; for example, models with multi-dimensional objective functions, including income redistribution, regional aid or development, or "social well-being."

The conclusions of this study are not encouraging. In a number of cases, inconsistencies were found between the ex ante evaluation procedures of the Corps of Engineers and those that would be derived from the basic efficiency model. In the case of navigation benefits, for example, the evaluation procedures applied by the agency (as required by law) have little, if any, relationship to an efficiency concept of benefits or any other benefit concept that has economic meaning. In the empirical case studies presented, ex post estimates of benefits often showed little relationship to their ex ante counterparts. On the basis of the few cases and the a priori analysis presented here, one could conclude that there is a serious bias incorporated into agency ex ante evaluation procedures, resulting in persistent overstatement of expected benefits. Similarly, in the analysis of project construction costs, enormous variance was found among projects in the relationship between estimated and realized costs. Although no persistent bias in estimation procedures was apparent, nearly 50 percent of the projects displayed realized costs that deviated by more than plus or minus 20 percent from ex ante projected costs. [1]

What then can we conclude from this analysis? First, and at a minimum, this study has demonstrated a need to seriously reappraise the procedures of benefit-cost analysis as practiced by the agencies. Unless procedures are constantly revised on the basis of performance feedback from existing undertakings, the credibility of ex ante analysis will, and should, be challenged. The serious discrepancies between projected and realized costs and benefits described in this study do little to instill confidence in current ex ante analysis.

Second, these results generate serious questions concerning the direction of recent efforts to revise planning and evaluation procedures in the water resources area. These efforts have largely neglected the need to improve the evaluation of primary benefits and costs and have concentrated on including several nonefficiency impacts, such as income distribution, regional growth, and secondary effects, in the basic evaluation model. Surely, knowledge of these nonefficiency effects is relevant to project appraisal and choice and information on them should be developed and presented to decision makers. However, given the serious shortfalls in the performance of ex ante benefit and cost estimation—an area where production functions are fairly well understood—the first order of business would seem to be improvement of these estimates before more esoteric impacts generated by linkages that are little understood are pushed full-blown into the basic ex ante evaluation model. Indeed, before more confidence can be placed in the benefit and cost estimates based on primary impacts, it seems almost ludicrous to develop complex procedures for building ex ante estimates of these elusive nonefficiency effects into formal criteria.[2] As W. B. Back has

---

[1] This estimate refers to the cost comparison based on current costs. See table 21.

[2] See A. Myrick Freeman III and Robert H. Haveman, "Benefit-Cost Analysis and Multiple Objectives: Current Issues in Water Resources Planning," *Water Resources Research*, vol. 6, no. 6 (December 1970), pp. 1533–39, for a further critique of the efforts to formalize multiple objective criteria in the planning process.

stated recently with respect to efforts to incorporate regional growth estimates into the basic model of public investment appraisal:

> The knowledge base necessary for developing defensible procedures for estimating the contributions of water projects to regional economic development does not exist. . . . Given this state of our knowledge, efforts to develop procedures related to "regional dynamics" of water resource development may be premature. A baby should not be expected to run before it has learned to walk.[3]

Finally, it would appear that a more substantial monitoring and ex post evaluation effort by agencies could lead to important improvements in benefit-cost procedures. Through such an effort, a basis for correcting persistent biases in existing ex ante estimation procedures would be obtained. Moreover, through regular and ongoing project monitoring and evaluation, much could be discovered about the little-known and vaguely understood relationships between public investments and changes in income distribution, regional growth, and environmental quality. At this time, obtaining increased knowledge of these relationships clearly must precede the development of comprehensive ex ante project evaluation criteria that incorporate these nonefficiency variables.[4]

---

[3] W. B. Back, "Estimating Contributions of Natural Resource Investments to Objectives in Regional Economic Development," *Journal of Agricultural Economics*, vol. 51, no. 5 (December 1969), pp. 1446–47.

[4] Gilbert White has also recently emphasized the need to undertake appraisal of the performance of completed works in order to better understand both the efficiency and nonefficiency impacts of water developments. He states: ". . . the analytical methods to determine effects, as in the case of income redistribution from building an irrigation scheme or impacts upon ecosystems from a new reservoir, are still imperfect. It is partly because few attempts have been made to apply what methods are available to the appraisal of completed works. The shelves are bursting with plans and with normative studies of optimal solutions. A few inches will suffice to record what is known, in fact, to have happened . . . ." Gilbert F. White, *Strategies of American Water Management* (University of Michigan Press, 1969), p. 14.

APPENDIX A

The Use of Land Values in the Ex Post Evaluation of Benefits of Flood Protection Investments

The use of land values in ex post project evaluation requires a comprehensive study of land values in the entire base region (including the floodplain) at both the time of project construction and the time of performance appraisal, as well as a reconstructed ex ante analysis that projects land value changes. The following equation provides the basis for evaluating the volume of the primary project benefits realized by the flood control investment and for comparing these benefits with those projected by ex ante estimation procedures. It assumes the use of an analogue region, a base region larger than, but encompassing, the floodplain, for estimating land value changes occurring without construction of the facility. For each category of land on the floodplain, the analyst must choose a similar land category off the floodplain but within the base region for comparative purposes.

If Z_i = difference between estimated realized project benefits and projected benefits on land category i,

V_i = land values on land category i,

c = year in which investment was undertaken,

n = year of efficiency performance appraisal,

f = locations in the floodplain,

b = nonfloodplain locations in the base area,

o = observed values,

p = projected values in reconstructed ex ante survey,

then the comparison of projected and realized project benefits on a particular category of land (Z_i) is given by:

$$Z_i = [\{V_n^{fo} - V_c^{fo}\} - \{V_n^{bo} - V_c^{bo}\}] - [\{V_n^{fp} - V_c^{fo}\} - \{V_n^{bp} - V_c^{bo}\}].$$

Given this equation as the conceptual basis for making a comparison of realized and projected project benefits, it must also be assumed that the *observed* rate of growth of the entire base area equals the rate of growth of the base area without the project, and that the rate of growth of the floodplain without the project would have coincided with the growth rate of the entire base area.

Because of the enormous data requirements for such an analysis, ex post evaluation relying on land value changes is a highly problematic empirical task. In addition, there are a number of reasons why such estimates of comparative

113

land value changes would fail to yield an accurate empirical estimate of the realized benefits from flood protection. Indeed, the performance conclusions suggested by the calculated Z may be in error because of the failure of any of its terms to accurately measure the appropriate variables. In particular, serious estimation errors are likely in the comparison of observed land value changes in the floodplain ($V_n^{fo} - V_c^{fo}$) and predicted land value changes in the floodplain ($V_n^{fp} - V_c^{fo}$). Measurement errors in these variables would be introduced if either (1) V_n^{fo} overestimated or underestimated true realized benefits or (2) V_n^{fp} overestimated or underestimated real benefits. Because an observed Z_i would imply either erroneous measurements of realized benefits or erroneous ex ante projections, the analyst would be unable to filter out the contribution of each error source to the observed value.

Because of the following rigidities and inherent measurement problems, the calculated value of Z may be difficult to interpret and, consequently, of limited value as an instrument for ex post evaluation:

V_n^{fo} would tend to be erroneously estimated because:

(1) Benefits from the reduction of flood damage to structures, such as the reduction in damages to highways, railroads, utilities, and other public facilities, are not reflected in land value changes.

(2) Indirect benefits isolated in case 3 discussed in the text are not reflected in changes in land values for lands on the floodplain.

(3) Observed land values become inflated by the increased demands of that incursion of the floodplain due to lack of information or misinformation concerning the extent of protection offered by the floodplain.

V_n^{fp} would tend to be erroneously estimated because:

(1) Projected annual benefits based on the cost of repairing damaged facilities to return them to their preflood value (as opposed to their preflood condition) have little empirical basis.

(2) The real costs of risk-bearing are difficult to empirically fold into the projected benefit estimate.[1]

(3) Intangible (yet real) outputs—reduction in loss of life, enhancement of the security of people, improvement of sanitation—are difficult to empirically fold into projected annual benefits.[2]

---

[1] See Robert C. Lind, "Flood Control Alternatives and the Economics of Flood Protection," *Water Resources Research*, vol. 3, no. 2 (Second Quarter, 1967), pp. 345–50.

[2] These social benefits are reflected in the land value of floodplain locations.

APPENDIX B

The 1964 Revision of Waterway Evaluation Procedures
by William Proxmire

In recent months, several members of Congress have criticized the Corps of Engineers' new and improved procedures for estimating the benefits to be derived from waterway projects. The Corps is under intense pressure from Congress to recommend projects which are primarily intended to inject massive federal funds into a congressman's district or state.

Now that the Corps has implemented a system which more accurately measures future benefits, it is only natural that it should come under congressional fire from legislators who are threatened with the loss of multimillion-dollar projects. Thus, I believe it is high time someone spoke out in support of the Corps efforts to spend our tax dollars wisely.

From the standpoint of society as a whole, the goal of all economic ventures is to obtain the maximum amount of goods and services at the lowest possible cost of resources. For instance, it would be senseless to build four waterways to do an amount of work that can be done equally well by one waterway: in this situation four water projects vastly increase costs but provide no additional benefit. In the same way, it makes no sense to build even one waterway if alternative modes of transportation can do the job with a smaller expenditure of society's resources. In order that proposed waterways shall conform to this goal of maximum production of goods and services at the least cost in resources, it is necessary to know, first, the amount of traffic that will be carried by the waterway and, second, whether this traffic will be carried more cheaply by water than by alternative modes of transportation. For, if we determine both the amount of traffic to be carried and whether it will be carried most cheaply by water, we can determine whether the proposed waterway or an alternative mode of transport will do the work at least cost.

Now, it is a certainty that the amount of traffic that will move via water depends in great part on the water rate as compared with the rate charged by competing modes of transportation, such as the railroads, the mode to which I shall refer here. Before altering its procedures, the Corps used to estimate the amount of traffic accruing to a potential waterway by comparing the current water rate

Excerpted from a speech delivered by Senator Proxmire on the floor of the Senate, June 20, 1966, and published in the *Congressional Record*, daily ed., September 29, 1966, pp. 23425–26.

with the current rail rate. The Corps would then calculate the benefit accruing to this waterway traffic by again using the difference between the current water and rail rates. To illustrate these bygone procedures, assume that at current rates shippers pay $2 to move a unit of traffic via water and $3 to ship it via rail. The Corps would calculate that the difference in rates would cause a certain amount of traffic to shift to water transportation—let us assume it would be 100 units. Each of these 100 units would save the $1 difference between the water and rail rates so that the total benefit accruing to the water traffic would be $100.

However, as many observers pointed out, these old procedures were seriously defective for at least two reasons. First, it was erroneous to use current rail and water rates to estimate the traffic that would move by waterway in the future. For, both railroads and water carriers are undergoing technological innovations which imply that in future years rates will be lower and that there will be a smaller spread between water rates and rail rates. Moreover, if and when a waterway comes into existence, rail rates will become lower entirely aside from improvements in technology. This is so because railroads charge what the traffic will bear, a method of pricing which, in the absence of competition, creates a very large gap between the railroad's costs and the rates it charges. When a waterway comes into existence, the competition it provides forces the railroad to bring its rates more into line with its costs: for example, the rail rate on petroleum shipments from Portland, Oregon, to Florida fell by 38 percent after a competing portion of the Columbia River became navigable. Thus, since technological improvements and waterway competition insure that future rates will be closer to water rates than is true currently, the former Corps practice of using current rates to estimate future waterway traffic resulted in an overestimation of such traffic. In terms of our previous example, where there was a $1 difference between current rail and water rates and where the spread caused 100 units of traffic to move via water, in the future there will be a smaller spread between rail and water rates and, everything else being equal, less than 100 units will move via water.

In addition to overestimating the amount of traffic which would move via water, the Corps' old procedures also overestimated the benefit accruing because traffic is carried by water rather than rail. In this connection, it must be understood that real social benefit only arises if the water project provides its service at a lower cost of real social resources. In other words, there is benefit only if less steel, concrete, labor, management skill, and so forth are used up in carrying traffic by water than in carrying traffic via rail. Therefore, the ideal way to measure benefit would be to measure the value of steel, concrete, and other costs required by water transportation and compare this with the value of the steel, concrete, and so forth required by rail transportation. However, the plain fact of the matter is that at present there is no satisfactory method for producing a sufficiently exact comparison of real water and rail costs. It is necessary, therefore, to fall back on the best substitute method available: benefit—or the saving in real costs —is computed by comparing water rates with rail rates.

There was, however, a threefold problem with the Corps' previous procedure of comparing current water rates with current rail rates to estimate future benefit. First, since the amount of traffic was overestimated, so was the benefit. Second, since, as we have seen, charging what the traffic will bear causes current rail rates to be far above current real rail costs, the amount of future cost saving is exaggerated when the current water rate is subtracted from the bloated current rail rate. Third, since technological progress will, in the future, diminish the spread between real water costs and real rail costs, the amount of future cost saving is even further exaggerated by comparing current water and rail rates to estimate future benefit. In terms of our previous example, where the current water and rail rates were $2 and $3 respectively, the old procedures exaggerated benefit because, first, less than 100 units of traffic will move via water; second, the spread between the current $2 water rate and the bloated current $3 rail rate is greater than the spread between current costs; and third, in the future the spread between real costs will be even less than it is today.

I should now like to briefly recapitulate some of the salient points in the foregoing. Formerly, the Corps used current water and rail rates to estimate the future traffic and benefits of a proposed waterway. However, because of technological improvements in rail travel as well as competition from the proposed waterway, in the future there will be a smaller spread between rail and water rates. There will also be a smaller spread between real rail costs and real water costs. For these reasons, the use of current rates to make predictions resulted in over-estimating both the amount of future traffic and the amount of future benefit accruing to waterways.

By its recent change in policy, however, the Corps has adopted more accurate and economically appropriate procedures for making estimates. The Corps now estimates the amount of traffic that will move on a future waterway by comparing the estimated future water rate with the estimated future rate which railroads will charge to meet the water competition—referred to as the water-compelled rail rate. It then measures benefit by the difference between the future water rate and the rail rate that would have been paid in the absence of waterway competition—the non-water-compelled rail rate. In terms of our previous example, one might find that the future water rate will be $1.75, the future water-compelled rail rate will be $2 and the future non-water-compelled rail rate will be $2.50. Under these conditions, fifty units of traffic will move by water and each unit will benefit by the difference between the $1.75 future water-compelled rate and the $2.50 rail rate that would have been paid in the absence of a waterway. I note parenthetically that the future non-water-compelled rail rate of $2.50 is lower than the current rail rate of $3 because of technological improvement but higher than the future water-compelled rail rate of $2 because of the lack of water competition.

The Corps' new procedures are far better than its old ones because the present procedures are based on more accurate approximations of future traffic, rates, and costs. We know that rates will not remain static and that current rates therefore do not reflect future ones. This means that a railway charging $3 to move a unit of traffic today would only charge, say, $2 in competition with a waterway, both because of technological advances and competitive pressures. The Corps, recognizing this built-in defect, is now using future rate estimates in arriving at both the amount of traffic which will move on a proposed waterway and the benefit to the national economy of the waterway. As a result, estimated waterway traffic, together with estimated benefits from the waterway, are substantially less. The Corps' new methods insure that, in making its decisions, Congress will have a much better idea of the value to society of its appropriations. Clearly, it is much better to calculate traffic and benefit by using reasonable predictions of future rates, as the Corps now does, than to use current rates, as the Corps formerly did, and as many congressional critics say they will continue to do.

APPENDIX C

List of Projects Studied in Chapter 5, by Category

Flood Control

Ball Mountain Reservoir, Vermont
Barre Falls Reservoir, Massachusetts
Bear Creek Reservoir, Pennsylvania
Bradford, Pennsylvania
Buffalo Bayou, Texas
Cape Girardeau, Missouri
Carthage, Missouri
Catlettsburg, Kentucky
Coyote Valley Reservoir, California
Devil, East Twin, Warm and Lytle Creeks, California
Eagle Gorge Reservoir, Washington
East Poplar Bluff and Poplar Bluff, Missouri
Hartford (Folly Brook), Connecticut
Little Missouri Rivers below Murfreesboro, Arkansas
Little Sioux River and Tributaries, Iowa
*Lower San Joaquin River and Tributaries, California
McCook Lake, South Dakota
Otterbrook Reservoir, New Hampshire
Painted Rock Dam, Iowa
Riverside Levees, California
Rough River Reservoir, Kentucky
San Antonio and Chino Creeks, California
Sioux Falls, South Dakota
Woonsocket, Rhode Island

Multi-Purpose

Cougar Reservoir, Oregon
Fort Gaines, Georgia
Hartwell Reservoir, Georgia and South Carolina
Hills Creek Reservoir, Oregon
Ice Harbor Lock and Dam, Washington
McGee Bend Dam, Texas

Navigation

Ashtabula Harbor, Ohio
Bayou Coden, Alabama
Bayou La Battre, Alabama
Bayous La Loutre, St. Malo, and Yscloskey, Louisiana
Beaufort Harbor (Taylor Creek), North Carolina
Brady Island Channel, Houston Ship Channel, Texas
Channel Back Sound to Lookout Bight, North Carolina
Charleston Harbor, South Carolina
Columbia River at the Mouth, Washington
Coos Bay, Oregon
Dauphine Island Bay, Alabama
Davis Creek, Virgina
Deep Creek, Virginia
Fairport Harbor, Ohio
Hendricks Harbor, Maine
*Hildebrand Lock and Dam, Monongahela River, Pennsylvania and West
    Virginia
Honga River and Tar Bay, Maryland
Indian River Inlet to Rehobeth Bay, Delaware
Island Creek, Maryland
Little River, Cuyahoga Island, New York
Lubec Channel, Maine
Metlakatla Harbor, Alaska
Mobile Harbor, Alabama
Nanticoke River (including Northwest Fork), Delaware, Maryland
Nawiliwili Harbor, Hawaii
Neah Bay, Washington
New River, Florida
Northport Harbor, New York
Patchoque River, Connecticut
Port Royal Harbor, South Carolina
Portsmouth Harbor and Piscataqua River, New Hampshire
Quimby Creek, Virginia
Redondo Beach and Harbor, California
Rhodes Point to Tylertown, Maryland
Rice Creek, Florida
Richmond Harbor, California
Rock Hall Harbor, Maryland
Rollinson Channel, North Carolina
St. Augustine (San Sebastian), Florida
St. Patricks Creek, Maryland
Seward Refuge Harbor, Alaska
*Small Boat Harbor, Rock Island, Illinois
Smith Creek, North Carolina
Tacoma Harbor, Washington

Tampa Harbor, Florida
Tillamook Bay and Bar, Oregon
Town River, Massachusetts
Turtle Cove, Texas
Twitch Cove and Big Thoroughfare River, Maryland
Umpqua River, Oregon
Urbana Creek, Virginia
Wallace Channel, North Carolina
Whitings Creek, Virginia
Wilmington Harbor, North Carolina
Wrangell Harbor, Alaska

Shore Protection

Presque Isle, Pennsylvania

* Not included in list of projects adjusted for price change.

INDEX

THE JOHNS HOPKINS PRESS

Composed in Times Roman text and display
by Monotype Composition Company

Printed on 60-lb. Sebago MF, Text Color
by Universal Lithographers, Inc.

Bound in Interlaken Seta
by L. H. Jenkins, Inc.

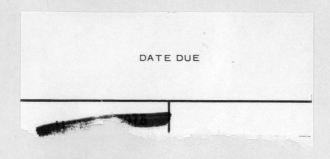

DATE DUE